10 Minute Guide to QuickBooks™

Linda Flanders

alpha
books

A Division of Prentice Hall Computer Publishing
11711 North College, Carmel, Indiana 46032 USA

To Scott, for your continued support and encouragement.

©1992 by Alpha Books

International Standard Book Number: 1-56761-113-3
Library of Congress Catalog Card Number: 92-74263

95 94 93 92   8 7 6 5 4 3 2 1

Interpretation of the printing code: the rightmost double-digit number is the year of the book's printing; the rightmost single-digit number is the number of the book's printing. For example, a printing code of 92-1 shows that the first printing of the book occurred in 1992.

Publisher: *Marie Butler-Knight*
Managing Editor: *Elizabeth Keaffaber*
Product Development Manager: *Lisa A. Bucki*
Acquisitions Manager: *Stephen R. Poland*
Production Editor: *Lisa C. Hoffman*
Manuscript Editors: *Barry Childs-Helton, San Dee Phillips, Audra Gable*
Editorial Assistant: *Hilary J. Adams*
Cover Design: *Dan Armstrong*
Designer: *Amy Peppler-Adams*
Indexer: *Johnna VanHoose*
Production Team: *Tim Cox, Mark Enochs, Joelynn Gifford, Tim Groeling, Phil Kitchel, Tom Loveman, Michael J. Nolan, Joe Ramon, Carrie Roth, Mary Beth Wakefield, Kelli Widdifield*

Special thanks to C. Herbert Feltner for ensuring the technical accuracy of this book.

Screen reproductions in this book were created by means of the program Collage Plus from Inner Media, Inc., Hollis, NH.

Printed in the United States of America

Contents

Introduction

Owning a small business—or doing the bookkeeping for a small business—can be a tremendous task. But if you've just purchased QuickBooks for your computer to automate your business's finances, you'll soon find out how easily and swiftly you can perform day-to-day bookkeeping tasks. Until now, all you've heard about QuickBooks was that it is a program that allows business owners and bookkeepers to manage the finances of a small business. A few things are certain:

- You need to learn the program quickly.

- You need to identify and learn only the tasks necessary to accomplish your particular goals.

- You need a clear-cut, plain-English guide to learn about the basic features of the program.

The *10 Minute Guide to QuickBooks* is designed to teach you the operations you need in short, easy-to-understand lessons that can be completed in 10 minutes or less.

The 10 Minute Guide series is a new approach to learning computer programs. Instead of trying to teach you everything about a particular software product (and ending up with an 800-page book in the process), the 10 Minute Guide teaches you only about the often-used features.

Each 10 Minute Guide contains more than 20 short lessons. The 10 Minute Guide teaches you about programs without relying on technical jargon—you'll find only plain English used to explain the procedures in this book. With straightforward, easy-to-follow steps and special artwork (icons) to call your attention to important tips and definitions, the 10 Minute Guide makes learning a new software program fast and easy.

The following icons help you find your way around the *10 Minute Guide to QuickBooks:*

 **Timesaver Tips** offer shortcuts and hints for using the program more effectively.

 Plain English icons identify definitions of new terms.

 Panic Button icons appear at places where new users often run into trouble.

Additionally, a table of quick keys (included at the end of the book) shows you the key combinations that access QuickBooks' options and features instantly.

These specific conventions will help you find your way around QuickBooks as easily as possible:

1. Numbered steps	Step-by-step instructions are highlighted with bold numbers in color so you can find basic QuickBooks procedures quickly.
What you type	The keys you press will appear in color. The information you type will be in bold, color computer type.

What you see on-screen   The text you see on-screen will appear in computer type.

Menu names   The names of QuickBooks menus, options, and activities are displayed with the first letter capitalized.

Menu selections   The letters you press to pull down menus and activate menu options are printed in bold type.

The *10 Minute Guide to QuickBooks* is organized in lessons that range from basic startup to more advanced customizing features. Remember, however, that nothing in this book is difficult. Most users want to start at the beginning of the book with the lesson on starting QuickBooks, and progress (as time allows) through the lessons sequentially.

Who Should Use the *10 Minute Guide to QuickBooks?*

The *10 Minute Guide to QuickBooks* is for anyone who:

- Needs to learn QuickBooks quickly.
- Doesn't have a lot of time to spend learning a new program.
- Wants to find out quickly whether QuickBooks will meet his or her computer needs.
- Wants a clear, concise guide to the most important features of the QuickBooks program.

You say your time is important to you, and that you need to make the most of it. The *10 Minute Guide to QuickBooks* will help you learn this extremely powerful program in a fraction of the time you might ordinarily spend struggling with new software.

What Is QuickBooks?

QuickBooks is a small-business bookkeeping program that helps you track the income and expenses of the business. If you are familiar with Quicken, the popular personal book-keeping package, you'll find that QuickBooks works much the same way. You can even convert your Quicken data files to QuickBooks in just seconds, without disturbing your Quicken data. With QuickBooks, you can:

- Write and print checks.
- Write and print customer invoices.
- Keep company lists.
- Reconcile your checking account.
- Track your accounts receivable and payable.
- Create and print reports.

Trademarks

All terms mentioned in this book that are known to be service marks are listed below. In addition, terms suspected of being trademarks or service marks have been appropriately capitalized. Alpha Books cannot attest to the accuracy of this information. Use of a term in this book should not be regarded as affecting the validity of any trademark or service mark.

QuickBooks and Quicken are trademarks of Intuit.

Lesson 1

Getting Started with QuickBooks

In this lesson, you'll learn how to start and end a typical QuickBooks session. You will also learn how to use the Main menu and various pull-down menus.

Starting QuickBooks

If you installed QuickBooks according to the instructions on the inside front cover of this book, follow these steps:

1. Turn on your computer.

2. At the c:> prompt, type QB and press Enter. A QuickTrainer message is displayed the first time you start QuickBooks.

3. Press Esc to remove the QuickTrainer message from the screen.

After the QuickTrainer message is removed, the Main menu appears, as shown in Figure 1.1.

1

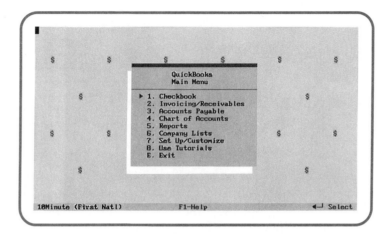

Figure 1.1 The QuickBooks Main menu.

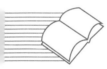

QuickTrainer QuickBooks' on-screen tutor displays messages when QuickBooks determines that you may be having difficulties (when you take no action within a few seconds). Press Esc to remove QuickTrainer messages from your screen. QuickTrainer is explained in more detail in Lesson 3.

Starting QuickBooks the First Time When you start QuickBooks for the first time, you must set up your company and a checking account before you can begin using the program to perform your bookkeeping tasks. You learn how to set up your company and a checking account in Lesson 2.

Selecting Menu Options

You can select program options from the Main menu using one of the following methods:

- Press the number that corresponds to the activity or option you want to select. For example, to select the Reports option from the Main menu, press 5.

- Using the Up and Down arrow keys, move the arrow to the activity or option you want to select. Press Enter. For example, to select the Checkbook option from the Main menu, move the arrow to the Checkbook line and press Enter.

- Press a quick key (Ctrl-key) combination. Quick keys are listed on the inside back cover. For example, to select the Chart of Accounts option, press Ctrl-A.

- Position the mouse pointer on the option or activity you want to select, and click the left mouse button.

Note that when some of the Main menu options are selected, QuickBooks displays a second menu with additional options. For example, when you select the Checkbook option, QuickBooks displays the Checkbook menu with three additional options: Write/Print Checks, Check Register, and Reconcile. Use the same procedures as explained above to select options from the second menu.

Using Pull-Down Menus

After you've selected one of the Main menu options, QuickBooks displays the opening screen for that activity. Some screens offer pull-down menus to access program options.

3

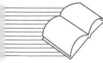

Pull-Down Menu   A menu that remains hidden within a menu bar until you use the keyboard or mouse to open or *pull down* the complete menu. The complete menu contains additional options, features, and functions of the program. After you access the pull-down menu, you may select any of the options. Some options available from a pull-down menu, however, may be selected using quick keys (as listed on the inside back cover). When a quick key is available, it is not necessary to access the pull-down menu first. Simply press the quick key to make your selection.

To access a pull-down menu from the menu bar that appears at the top of the screen, press the function key that appears to the left of the pull-down menu name. For example, to access the Find/Edit pull-down menu (shown in Figure 1.2) from the Write Checks screen, press F3.

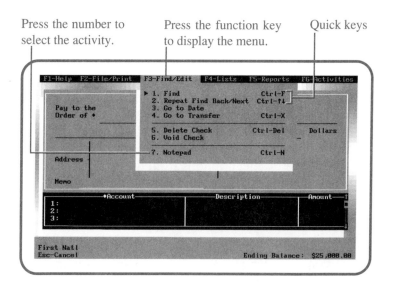

Figure 1.2   The Find/Edit pull-down menu, accessed by pressing F3 from the Write Checks screen.

To select an option or activity from a QuickBooks pull-down menu, press the number that appears to the left of that option or activity. For example, to select the Delete Check option from the Find/Edit pull-down menu shown in Figure 1.2, press 5.

Using Quick Keys   Many options and activities in pull-down menus can be selected using quick keys. A *quick key* is a combination of the Ctrl key and a letter key pressed simultaneously. There is no need to access the pull-down menu to use quick keys. Simply press the quick keys from a register screen, the Write Checks screen, or the Write In-voices screen.

Using the Keyboard

Your keyboard can be used to select menu options and commands, and to move around QuickBooks screens.

Throughout the remainder of this book, the term *select*, for keyboard users, will mean one of the following:

- Press the number that appears to the left of the option or activity name.

- Move the arrow to the menu or option name and press Enter.

Using a Mouse

Any Microsoft-compatible mouse can be used to select menu options, pull down menus, move around the screen, or select items from lists. To perform most QuickBooks operations with a mouse, simply point and click.

Point and Click   To point to an item on the screen, move the mouse on your desktop or mouse pad so that the mouse pointer points to the item on the screen. Then press and release (click) the left mouse button.

This book will explain *keyboard* steps for performing operations in QuickBooks. Therefore, if you are using a mouse, note the following procedures:

Operation	Mouse Procedure
Choose an item from a list	Double-click.
Scroll up or down a register or list	Hold down the left mouse button on a transaction or list item, and move the mouse up or down. Position the mouse pointer on the upper or lower scroll arrow, and hold down the left mouse button.
Move to the next or previous transaction or list item	Click the arrows on the vertical scroll bar.
Page up or page down a screen	Click the vertical scroll bar above or below the scroll box.

Move to the next check or invoice	Click the down arrow below the check voucher or invoice.
Move to the preceding check or invoice	Click the up arrow below the check voucher or invoice.
Move right or left in a report screen	Click the horizontal scroll bar to the right or left of the scroll box, respectively.

Figure 1.3 shows the vertical scroll bar arrow and box from a register screen.

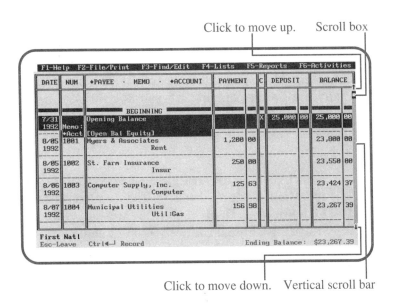

Figure 1.3   The vertical scroll bar arrow and the vertical scroll box.

For the remainder of this book, the term *select* (for mouse users) will mean to point and click on the option or item.

Backing Up Your Company Files

Although QuickBooks automatically saves the data in your company file from your work session when you edit, it's wise to keep backup copies of all data. To make a backup copy of your current company file before exiting QuickBooks, follow these steps:

1. Press Esc to return to the Main menu (if necessary).

2. Press Ctrl-E at the Main menu to select the backup option.

3. Place your backup disk in drive A or B.

4. Type the drive letter for your backup disk. Press Enter to begin the backup process.

5. QuickBooks displays a message that the current company file was backed up successfully.

6. Press Enter to exit QuickBooks.

Backing Up Without Exiting   Press Ctrl-B from the Main menu to back up files without exiting QuickBooks. Then select the company file you want to back up, and follow steps 3 and 4 above.

Exiting QuickBooks

To exit QuickBooks and save your company files automatically:

1. Press Esc to return to the Main menu (if necessary).

2. Press E to select Exit from the Main menu. QuickBooks saves the data in your company file and returns you to the DOS prompt.

Unsaved Data   *Do not exit QuickBooks by turning off your computer*—data from your current work session will not be saved. Although QuickBooks reconstructs some files the next time it is used, complete reconstruction of company files is not possible.

In the next lesson, you will learn how to set up your QuickBooks system by setting up your company and your checking account, and how to set up QuickBooks to print to your printer.

Lesson 2

Setting Up
QuickBooks

In this lesson, you will learn how to set up your company file and a checking account, and how to set up QuickBooks to print to your printer.

Setting Up Your Company

You cannot do any work in QuickBooks until you create a company file that QuickBooks can use to store your data.

Company File QuickBooks stores your data in a company file. You must define your company before QuickBooks can create a company file. QuickBooks stores your chart of accounts, transactions, and company lists in your company file. You can add as many company files in QuickBooks as you may need, however, you can only work in one company file at a time.

To set up your company file, follow these steps:

1. From the Main menu, select the Set Up/Customize option.

2. QuickBooks displays the Set Up/Customize menu. Choose the Select/Add a Company option.

3. If no other company files exist, QuickBooks displays the Add New Company window shown in Figure 2.1. Proceed to step 4.

   If other company files exist, QuickBooks displays the Select/Set Up Company window. Press F7 to access the Actions menu and then select the Add New option. QuickBooks displays the Add New Company window. Proceed to step 4.

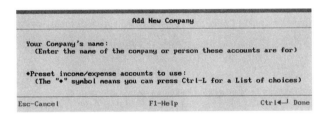

Figure 2.1   Use the Add New Company window to set up your company file.

4. Type your company name and press Enter. Company names can be up to 30 characters long and can include numbers, letters, and characters in any combination (including spaces).

5. At the Preset income/expense accounts to use field, press Ctrl-L to see a list of business types.

6. Use the Up and Down arrow keys to scroll through the list of business types; move the arrow next to the business type that best describes your company. Press Enter.

7. QuickBooks returns to the Add New Company window. Press Ctrl-Enter or F10.

8. QuickBooks displays the Creating Company Files for window with the name of your company.

   Note that QuickBooks changes the name of your company to conform with DOS file name rules, eliminating spaces and illegal characters such as \.

9. Make any necessary changes to the file name or directory, and press Ctrl-Enter or F10 to create your company file.

10. QuickBooks displays the Chart Of Accounts window (see Figure 2.2) for your company file. This window displays the preset list of accounts you chose in step 6. From the Chart of Accounts, you can create your checking account (as explained later in this lesson).

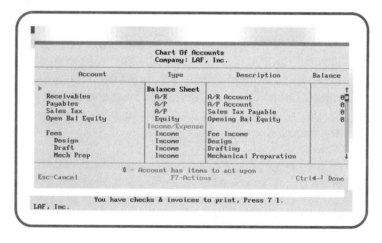

Figure 2.2   The Chart of Accounts for your company file.

Selecting a Business Type   When you select a business type, QuickBooks automatically adds a preset list of income, expense, and balance sheet (asset and liability) accounts to your company file. You can later add, edit, or delete accounts in the list. See Lesson 5 to learn how to work with accounts.

Filling in List Fields   A black diamond displayed next to a field name represents a list field. To fill in a list field, press Ctrl-L from the list field (or click on the black diamond) to display a list of items from which to choose. Then use the Up and Down arrow keys to point to the item you want to select, and press Enter.

Converting Quicken Data to QuickBooks

You can easily convert your Quicken data to QuickBooks. QuickBooks copies your Quicken accounts and data to your company file. Note that QuickBooks creates an accounts receivable account, an accounts payable account, and a sales-tax payable account in your company file—automatically—regardless of whether these accounts were present in Quicken.

To convert your Quicken data to QuickBooks:

1. Select the Set Up/Customize option from the Main menu.

2. QuickBooks displays the Set Up/Customize window. Select the Add Company Using Data from Quicken option.

13

3. Enter the directory where your Quicken data files are stored, and press Enter.

4. If the Quicken directory contains more than one file, use the Up and Down arrow keys to move the arrow to the file you want to convert, and then press Enter.

5. In the Enter Company Name window (displayed next), type a name for your QuickBooks company (up to 30 characters long) and press Enter.

6. QuickBooks displays the Creating Company Files window. Change the company file name or the directory if necessary. Press Ctrl-Enter or F10 to create a company file from the Quicken data file.

Quicken Data Unchanged   Your Quicken data file remains intact and unchanged when you convert the file to QuickBooks; there are now two distinct files. You may continue to use your Quicken data file without affecting the data in your QuickBooks company file.

Creating a Checking Account

The transactions you enter in QuickBooks have their greatest and widest impact on the checking account. Therefore, you must create a checking account before you can begin using QuickBooks to enter transactions. To create a checking account in QuickBooks:

1. Select Chart of Accounts from the Main menu.

2. QuickBooks displays the Chart Of Accounts window for your company. (Note that if you just set up your company file, the Chart Of Accounts window may already be displayed.)

3. Press F7 to display the Actions menu. This menu includes all actions that can be performed in the chart of accounts (add new, delete, and so forth).

4. Select the Add New option. QuickBooks displays the Select Type of Account To Add window.

5. Use the Up and Down arrow keys to move the arrow to the Checking account type, and press Enter.

6. QuickBooks displays the Add New Checking Account window shown in Figure 2.3.

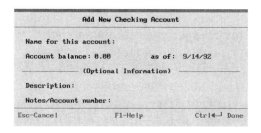

```
                    Add New Checking Account

    Name for this account :

    Account balance: 0.00          as of :  9/14/92
                    (Optional Information)

    Description:

    Notes/Account number :
    Esc-Cancel              F1-Help           Ctrl⏎ Done
```

Figure 2.3   Use the Add New Checking Account window to describe your checking account.

7. Type a name for the checking account, using up to 15 characters (including numbers, letters, and spaces). Press Enter.

8. Type the account balance as of the date that you will specify in the next step.

9. Type the date that you start using your QuickBooks system, or the date that you want reflected in your QuickBooks system as the starting date. Press Enter.

10. Type a description of the checking account and press Enter.

11. Type the account number (or any notes that describe the account) and press Enter.

12. Press Ctrl-Enter or F10 to create the checking account and add it to your chart of accounts.

Entering an Opening Balance Determining the opening balance for your checking account depends on how much financial history you want to enter in your QuickBooks system. If you want to start writing checks right away, without entering historical data, enter the ending balance from your last bank statement and use the current date as the opening (or "as of") date. Then enter any uncleared transactions or transactions that occurred between the last bank statement date and your "as of" date. If you want QuickBooks to reflect all activity from the beginning of the year, enter the ending balance in your account (as shown on your previous year-end balance sheet); then enter the first date of your fiscal year (usually January 1) as the "as of" date. Then enter all transactions that occurred from the beginning of the year to the date you started using QuickBooks. (You will learn how to enter transactions in the Check Register in Lesson 9.)

Setting Up QuickBooks for Your Printer

Before you can print checks, invoices, reports, or company lists with QuickBooks, you must tell QuickBooks what type of printer you are using. You can set up QuickBooks to print to one or two printers. To set up QuickBooks to work with your printer:

1. Press Esc to return to the Main menu (if necessary).

2. Select the Set Up/Customize option from the Main menu.

3. QuickBooks displays the Set Up/Customize menu. Select the Set Up Printers option.

4. QuickBooks displays two printers: printer 1 and printer 2. Press 1 to select Printer 1 or press 2 to select Printer 2. If the name of your printer is already shown next to printer 1 or 2, you don't need to do anything further; QuickBooks is already set up to work with your printer.

5. QuickBooks displays the Set Up Printer (1 or 2) window.

6. At the Printer name field, press Ctrl-L to display the Printer List. Use the Up and Down arrow keys to select a printer from the list, and press Enter.

7. QuickBooks returns to the Set Up Printer window. The printer port and normal printing styles for checks, invoices, and reports are displayed. You can make changes to any of the fields if necessary.

8. Press Ctrl-Enter or F10 to save the printer settings. If you don't want to set up a second printer, press Esc twice to return to the QuickBooks Main menu.

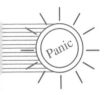

Your Printer Not Listed If you don't find your printer brand or model on the Printer List, refer to your printer manual to see whether your printer emulates a printer that is listed, and select that printer. If your printer does not emulate a printer on the list, call Intuit Technical Support for help with setting up an unlisted printer.

In the next lesson, you will learn how to use QuickBooks' on-screen Help system.

Lesson 3
Getting Help

In this lesson, you will learn how to use QuickBooks' on-screen Help system.

Using QuickBooks' Help System

QuickBooks offers a fully indexed, topical Help system. To access a QuickBooks Help screen, follow these steps:

1. From anywhere in QuickBooks, press F1. QuickBooks displays a window of information about the current screen.

2. If a topic within the information window is shown in boldface or color, you can access an additional Help window for information on only that topic; just move the cursor to the topic and press Enter. For example, in Figure 3.1, you see the Help window displayed from the Chart of Accounts.

   If you move the cursor to the Add a balance sheet account line and pressed Enter, QuickBooks displays a Help window with information on how to add a balance sheet account to the Chart of Accounts.

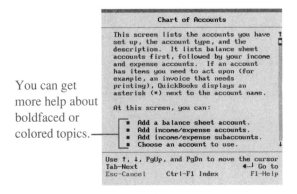

You can get more help about boldfaced or colored topics.

Figure 3.1   The Chart of Accounts Help window.

3. To remove the Help window from the screen, press Esc.

Using the Help Index

QuickBooks' Help system is indexed by topic. To locate a topic using the Help index, follow these steps:

1. Press Ctrl-F1 from anywhere in QuickBooks.

2. QuickBooks displays the Help Index. Move around the Help Index using the Up and Down arrow keys, the PgUp and PgDn keys, or the Tab key.

3. Use the following keys to locate topics:

   Tab moves to the next boldface or color topic.

   Shift-Tab moves to the preceding boldface or color topic.

   An alphabet key moves to the first topic that begins with that letter.

Ctrl-F displays the Find window; search for a word or phrase by typing it.

Backspace returns to the Help message you just left.

4. When you've located the topic you need help with, press Enter to display the Help window for that topic.

Accessing Help Table of Contents   QuickBooks' basic tasks are listed as a table of contents. To access this list, highlight the Table of Contents line at the beginning of the Help Index, and press Enter. Select the task with which you need help, and press Enter to display its Help window.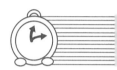

Using QuickTrainer

QuickTrainer is QuickBooks' "tutor for humans." The first time you start QuickBooks, you see a QuickTrainer message on your screen that assists you with the initial steps of registering your software, setting up your company, and setting up a checking account. At other times, if QuickBooks senses that you need help (because of a lag in response time), a QuickTrainer message is displayed to help you. QuickTrainer messages are similar to Help window messages and use the same keys to select topics.

When a QuickTrainer message is displayed and you no longer need it, press Esc to remove the message. During the current work session, QuickTrainer messages appear automatically only once at any one place in the program. If necessary, however, you can recall a QuickTrainer message by pressing Ctrl-Q. You can recall QuickTrainer messages as often as necessary during your work session.

Using Tutorials to Learn QuickBooks

QuickBooks provides an overview of the program and how to perform bookkeeping tasks through an on-screen tutorial. QuickBooks also provides sample company data you can use to go through the Quick Tour section of your QuickBooks manual. To use the QuickBooks tutorial, follow these steps:

1. Select the Use Tutorials option from the Main menu.

2. QuickBooks displays the Use Tutorials menu. Select the QuickBooks Overview option. If you need help getting started, select the Getting Started option. If you want to see how to use QuickBooks to write and print invoices, select the Invoicing option.

   To load the sample company data, follow these steps:

1. Select the Use Tutorials option from the Main menu.

2. QuickBooks displays the Use Tutorials menu. Select the Get Sample Company Data option.

3. When the data is ready to use, QuickBooks displays Sample Data Company in the lower left corner of the screen.

4. Press Esc to return to the Main menu.

   To remove the sample company data and access your own company file, follow these steps:

1. Select Exit from the Main menu.

2. QuickBooks returns to DOS. Start QuickBooks again by typing QB.

3. Select the Set Up/Customize option from the Main menu.

4. QuickBooks displays the Set Up/Customize window. Choose the Select/Add a Company option.

5. QuickBooks displays the Select/Set Up Company window. Use the Up and Down arrow keys to point to the company file you want to use. Press Enter.

In the next lesson, you will learn how to use QuickBooks' on-screen calculator.

Lesson 4

Using the Calculator

In this lesson, you'll learn how to use QuickBooks' on-screen calculator.

You can use the QuickBooks calculator any time you're working in the program. It can help you total multiple bills from the same vendor, verify credit statement totals, compute interest charges, and so forth. For convenience, use the on-screen calculator in place of your desktop model.

Accessing the Calculator

To access the QuickBooks calculator, follow these steps:

1. From a register, the Write Checks screen, or the Write Invoices screen, press F6 to access the Activities pull-down menu.

2. Select the Calculator option to display the QuickBooks calculator (as shown in Figure 4.1).

Quick Access You can access the on-screen calculator at any time in QuickBooks, simply by pressing Ctrl-C.

Figure 4.1   The QuickBooks calculator.

Using the Calculator

The on-screen calculator adds, subtracts, multiplies, and divides numbers. To use the calculator, follow these steps:

1. Access the QuickBooks calculator, as explained earlier in this lesson.

2. Enter the first number in your calculation. What you enter appears in the cursor line until you press an arithmetic sign or Enter.

3. Press one of the following signs:

    +   To add a number.

    –   To subtract a number.

    /   To divide a number.

    *   To multiply a number.

25

You can also use the mouse to select arithmetic signs. Just position the mouse pointer on the desired sign and click.

4. Enter the other numbers and arithmetic signs to continue your calculation.

5. Press Enter to complete and total your calculation.

Chain Calculations   To enter the last total calculated (after you have pressed Enter) in a subsequent calculation, press + or *, and QuickBooks enters the last total amount as the first number in your next calculation.

Clearing the Calculator   To clear the last calculation from the calculator, press C to select the Clear option.

Calculating Percentages

To add or subtract a percentage to or from a number, follow these steps:

1. Enter the number to which you want to add (or from which you want to subtract) a percentage.

2. Press + to add or – to subtract.

3. Enter the percentage that you want to add or subtract.

4. Type the % sign or click on % to convert the last number entered to a percentage and complete the calculation.

Pasting (Copying) Calculations

Using the Paste feature, you can enter the calculated amount from the on-screen calculator into an amount field in the QuickBooks program. To paste or copy a calculated amount into QuickBooks, follow these steps:

1. Position the cursor on the Amount field to which you want to paste a calculated number.

2. Press Ctrl-C to access the QuickBooks calculator.

3. Perform your calculation.

4. To copy the calculated amount to the amount field, press F9 to select Paste. After pasting the amount, QuickBooks clears the calculator from the screen.

Closing the Calculator

When you finish using the calculator, simply press Esc to clear the screen. The last calculation you performed will appear the next time you access the calculator during the current work session.

In the next lesson, you will learn how to work with the Chart of Accounts.

Lesson 5
Working with Accounts

In this lesson, you will learn how to add, edit, and delete accounts in your Chart of Accounts.

Exploring the Chart of Accounts

When you set up your company file, QuickBooks creates a Chart of Accounts based on the business type you select. *Chart of accounts* is an accounting term that refers to the list of accounts you use to classify your day-to-day transactions. Each transaction you enter in QuickBooks should be assigned to an account, so that you know exactly the types of expenses your business is incurring—and from where you are generating business income. The Chart of Accounts includes balance sheet, income, and expense accounts.

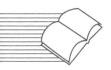

Balance Sheet Accounts Accounts affecting your company's net worth; three types are asset, liability, and owner's equity accounts. *Assets* are cash or noncash resources (accounts receivable, office equipment, land, patents, and so on). *Liabilities* are creditors' claims against your business's assets (accounts payable, credit card balances, working capital, real estate loans, and so on.). *Owner's*

equity represents the owner's interest in the business's assets; if your business is discontinued, owner's equity is what is left when all assets are sold and all liabilities are paid.

Accessing the Chart of Accounts

To access the Chart Of Accounts window, follow these steps:

1. Press Esc repeatedly to return to the QuickBooks Main menu.

2. Select Chart of Accounts from the Main menu. QuickBooks displays the Chart Of Accounts window shown in Figure 5.1.

```
                      Chart Of Accounts
                      Company: LAF, Inc.

        Account          Type          Description        Balance

                     Balance Sheet                                  ↑
  First Natl         Checking       Checking account       12,000▯
  Receivables        A/R            A/R Account                 0
  Payables           A/P            A/P Account                 0
  Sales Tax          A/P            Sales Tax Payable           0
  Open Bal Equity    Equity         Opening Bal Equity     12,000
                     Income/Expense
  Fees               Income         Fee Income
    Design           Income         Design
    Draft            Income         Drafting                    ↓

              * - Account has items to act upon
  Esc-Cancel              F7-Actions            Ctrl◄┘ Done
```

The Chart Of Accounts window is organized by Balance Sheet accounts first, then by Income and Expense accounts.

Figure 5.1 The Chart Of Accounts window.

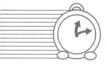

Finding Accounts in the Chart of Accounts Balance sheet accounts are listed first, followed by income and expense accounts. QuickBooks organizes accounts alphabetically within the appropriate section of the Chart of Accounts. The checking accounts, however, are always listed first. An asterisk (*) next to an account type indicates that you should take some action in that account.

Adding Accounts

Although QuickBooks sets up your Chart of Accounts for you, you may decide to add some income and expense accounts. You can add income and expense accounts as either first-level accounts or as subaccounts. (You learn how to add subaccounts later in this lesson.) To add an income or expense account to the Chart of Accounts:

1. Access the Chart Of Accounts window as explained earlier in this lesson.

2. Press F7 to display the Actions menu shown in Figure 5.2.

3. Select the Add New option from the Actions menu, or press Ctrl-Ins.

4. Use the Up and Down arrow keys to point to the account type you want to add (Income, Expense, or Subaccount), and press Enter. (Note that this lesson focuses on adding income and expense accounts. In Lessons 19 and 20, you'll learn how to add the balance sheet accounts discussed earlier in this lesson).

5. Depending on which account you chose to add in step 4, QuickBooks displays the Add New Income Account window or the Add New Expense Account window.

6. Type the account's name and press Enter. (Account names can include up to 15 characters, including numbers, letters, and spaces.)

7. Enter an optional account description.

8. Press Ctrl-Enter or F10 to add the account to the Chart Of Accounts window.

Press F7 to access the Actions menu.

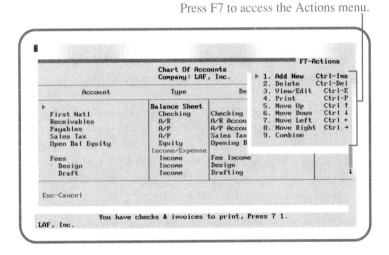

Figure 5.2 The Actions Menu from the Chart Of Accounts window.

Creating Subaccounts

Subaccounts further divide an account into second-, third-, fourth-, or fifth-level accounts. For example, if you want to divide the Repairs expense account so you can track separate expenses for repairing your building, office equipment, and computer equipment, you can set up three second-level expense subaccounts. Subaccounts are indented in the Chart of Accounts to show their relationship to first-level accounts.

To create a subaccount, follow these steps:

1. Access the Chart Of Accounts window as explained earlier in this lesson.

2. Use the Up and Down arrow keys to point to the account for which you want to create a subaccount.

3. Press F7 to display the Actions menu, and select the Add New option.

4. Use the Up and Down arrow keys to point to the Inc Subaccount or Exp Subaccount type (depending on the type of account you chose in step 2), and press Enter.

5. QuickBooks displays the Add New Income or Add New Expense Subaccount window.

6. Type the subaccount's name and press Enter. (Subaccount names can contain up to 15 characters, including numbers, letters, and spaces.)

7. Type a description, if desired.

8. Press Ctrl-Enter or F10 to create the subaccount.

Editing Accounts

To rename or change information for an income or expense account or subaccount, follow these steps:

1. Access the Chart Of Accounts window as explained earlier in this lesson.

2. Use the Up and Down arrow keys to point to the account you want to rename or change.

3. Press F7 to display the Actions menu and select the View/Edit option (or press Ctrl-E).

4. QuickBooks displays the View/Edit Account window. If you selected a subaccount in step 2, QuickBooks displays the View/Edit Subaccount window.

5. Type a new account name or a new account description.

6. Press Ctrl-Enter or F10 to save the changes to the account.

Deleting Accounts

You can delete an account from the Chart of Accounts at any time.

Be Careful When Deleting Accounts   When you delete an account that has been assigned to previous transactions or invoices, QuickBooks replaces the account in each prior transaction with a blank. To ensure that accounts are properly assigned to all transactions, you must go back and assign an account to each blank transaction when you delete the original account.

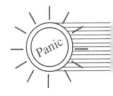

To delete an account or subaccount, follow these steps:

1. Access the Chart Of Accounts window as explained earlier in this lesson.

2. Use the Up and Down arrow keys to point to the account or subaccount you want to delete.

3. Press F7 to display the Actions menu and select the Delete option (or press Ctrl-Del).

4. QuickBooks displays a warning message and asks you to confirm the deletion of the account. Press Enter to delete the account or subaccount.

Deleting Accounts with Subaccounts When you delete an account that has subaccounts, QuickBooks also deletes all subaccounts.

Moving Accounts

You can change a first-level income or expense account to a subaccount, or change an income or expense subaccount to a first-level (or higher) account. This process is called *moving* accounts. You can also move a subaccount to another account. To move a first-level account to a subaccount:

1. Access the Chart Of Accounts window.

2. Use the Up and Down arrow keys to point to the first-level account you want to move.

3. Press and hold the Ctrl key while you press the Right arrow key (Ctrl-Right arrow). QuickBooks moves the

account to the subaccount position under the immediately preceding account. Now you can move the subaccount to a new location.

To move a subaccount to a higher-level account, follow these steps:

1. Access the Chart Of Accounts window.

2. Use the Up and Down arrow keys to point to the subaccount you want to move.

3. Press and hold the Ctrl key while you press the Left arrow key (Ctrl-Left arrow). QuickBooks moves the subaccount to the next higher level in the Chart of Accounts.

To move a subaccount to a different account, follow these steps:

1. Access the Chart Of Accounts window.

2. Use the Up and Down arrow keys to point to the subaccount you want to move.

3. Press and hold the Ctrl key while you press the Up or Down arrow keys to move the subaccount under a different account (Ctrl-Up arrow or Ctrl-Down arrow). When you release the Ctrl key, the move is completed.

Combining Accounts

You can combine or merge two accounts in one company file's Chart of Accounts. You can combine two income accounts, two expense accounts, or two balance sheet accounts. When you combine two accounts (A and B), QuickBooks deletes Account A, and only Account B remains. QuickBooks reassigns all Account A transactions to Account B.

To combine two accounts, follow these steps:

1. Access the Chart Of Accounts window.

2. Use the Up and Down arrow keys to point to the account you want to combine with another account.

3. Press F7 to display the Actions menu and select the Combine option.

4. QuickBooks displays the Select Account to Combine With window, which lists all the accounts with which you may combine the first account. Use the Up and Down arrow keys to point to the second account.

5. Press Ctrl-Enter to combine the accounts.

Printing the Chart of Accounts You can print the Chart of Accounts by selecting the Print option from the Actions menu, or by pressing Ctrl-P.

In the next lesson, you will learn how to set up the company lists you will use to enter transactions in QuickBooks.

Lesson 6

Using Company Lists

In this lesson, you will learn how to set up company lists, which you can use to fill in fields.

Working with Company Lists

QuickBooks provides several lists (called *company lists*) you can use to save time when entering transactions; they ensure that information is consistent in every transaction. Company lists store information about customers, vendors, employees, projects, and standard line items on invoices. You can also use customer lists to record customer and vendor types, payment terms, shipping and payment methods, and memos you include on invoices.

QuickBooks adds items to some company lists on the basis of the business type you selected when you set up your company file. You can add items, edit, or delete existing items from company lists at any time.

Accessing Company Lists

You can store various types of business information in company lists, and then use them to complete check, register, or invoice fields. QuickBooks provides the following company lists:

- **Payee List** Includes persons or firms you add to the Customer, Vendor, or Employee company lists.

- **Customer List** Customers' names and addresses.

- **Vendor List** Vendors' names and the current balance you owe to each vendor.

- **Employee List** Alphabetized list of employees and initials.

- **Items/Parts/Services** Information about the items, parts, or services your business provides.

- **Projects List** Lists projects, jobs, properties, locations, departments, or any other grouping specific to your small business.

- **Customer Types List** Types of customers with which you do business.

- **Vendor Types List** Types of vendors from which you purchase goods or services.

- **Payment Terms List** Lists the various payment terms you offer to your customers.

- **Shipping Methods List** Lists the methods your business uses to ship goods to customers.

- **Payments Methods List** Lists the methods of payment you accept from customers.

- **Invoice Memo List** Includes two-line memos you can print at the bottom of customer invoices.

To access one of the above company lists, follow these steps:

1. Press Esc to return to the QuickBooks Main menu (if necessary).

2. Select the Company Lists option from the Main menu.

3. QuickBooks displays the Select List window, as shown in Figure 6.1.

Use the Up and Down arrow keys to move the arrow (point) to the company list you want to access.

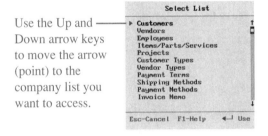

```
            Select List

      ▶ Customers                   ↑
        Vendors                     ▣
        Employees
        Items/Parts/Services
        Projects
        Customer Types
        Vendor Types
        Payment Terms
        Shipping Methods
        Payment Methods
        Invoice Memo                ↓

   Esc-Cancel  F1-Help   ◀┘ Use
```

Figure 6.1 The Select List window that includes all company lists.

4. Use the Up and Down arrow keys to point to the company list you want to access.

5. Press Enter to access the company list.

Adding to Company Lists

To add an item to a company list, follow these steps:

1. Access the company list to which you want to add an item (as explained earlier in this lesson).

2. Press F7 to display the Actions menu.

3. From the Actions menu, select the Add New option (or press Ctrl-Ins).

4. QuickBooks displays the Add New window. (Figure 6.2 shows the Add New Customer window displayed when you select the Add New option from the Customer List.)

Click here or press Ctrl-L to display a list.

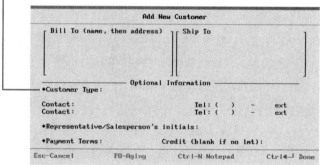

Figure 6.2   Use the Add New Customer window to add a new customer to the Customer List.

5. Fill in the Add New window. Note that you can make an entry in list fields (represented by a black diamond) by positioning the cursor on the field, pressing Ctrl-L (or

clicking on the black diamond) to display a list, and selecting an item from the list.

6. When the Add New window is complete, press Ctrl-Enter or F10 to add the item to the company list you selected in step 1.

Editing Items in a Company List

To change an item in a company list, follow these steps:

1. Access the company list in which you want to edit an item (as explained earlier in this lesson).

2. Press F7 to display the Actions menu.

3. From the Actions menu, select the View/Edit option (or press Ctrl-E).

4. QuickBooks displays the View/Edit window (which lists the same information as the Add New window seen in Figure 6.2).

5. Position the cursor on the field you want to edit, and type over the existing information.

   Note that you can change an entry in list fields (represented by a black diamond) by positioning the cursor on the field, pressing Ctrl-L or clicking on the black diamond to display a list, and selecting another item from the list.

6. When you have made the appropriate changes in the View/Edit window, press Ctrl-Enter or F10.

Deleting an Item from a Company List

Why Can't I Delete?   QuickBooks will not allow you to delete existing customers from the Customer List if you have previously written invoices for that customer. You also cannot delete existing vendors from the Vendor List if you have entered bills from that vendor in the Accounts Payable register.

To delete an item from a company list, follow these steps:

1. Access the company list from which you want to delete an item (as explained earlier in this lesson).

2. Press F7 to display the Actions menu.

3. From the Actions menu, select the Delete option (or press Ctrl-D).

4. QuickBooks displays a warning that you are permanently deleting an item.

5. Press Enter to delete the item.

Printing a Company List

To print a company list, follow these steps:

1. Access the company list you want to print.

2. Press F7 to display the Actions menu.

3. From the Actions menu, select the Print option (or press Ctrl-P).

4. QuickBooks displays the Print List window.

5. If you are printing the Customer or Vendor List, fill in the Select specific customers or vendors field, the Print name and balance only field, and the Include customer or vendor transaction history field. For all other company lists, select the printer you want to use by pressing Ctrl-L at the Print to field and choosing a printer from the list.

6. Press Ctrl-Enter or F10 to print the company list.

7. If you typed Y in the Select specific customers or vendors field, QuickBooks displays the Customer or Vendor List window. Move the arrow to the customer or vendor you want to include in the printed company list. Then press the Spacebar to select the customer or vendor. Press Enter to print selected customers or vendors.

In the next lesson, you will learn how to use QuickBooks to write checks.

Lesson 7
Writing Checks

In this lesson, you will learn how to use QuickBooks to write checks.

Working with the Write Checks Screen

Checks you want to print using QuickBooks are written in the Write Checks screen. Checks you write are not printed until you tell QuickBooks to print them. (See Lesson 8 to learn how to print checks).

The Write Checks screen is similar to a blank check. Note that checks you write manually are not entered at the Write Checks screen; enter these check transactions in the Check Register. (See Lesson 9 to learn how to enter transactions in the Check Register.)

Accessing the Write Checks Screen

To access the Write Checks screen, follow these steps:

1. Press Esc to return to the QuickBooks Main menu (if necessary).

2. Select the Checkbook option from the Main menu.

3. QuickBooks displays the Checkbook menu. Select Write/Print Checks.

4. QuickBooks displays the Write Checks screen shown in Figure 7.1.

Click here or press Ctrl-L to display a list from a diamond field.

Enter a check amount here.

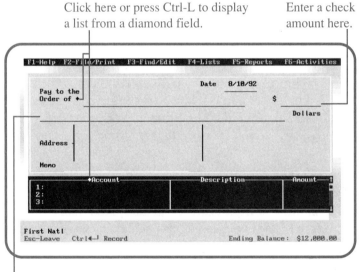

QuickBooks provides the written check amount automatically.

Figure 7.1   Use the Write Checks screen to write a check.

Quick Access   You can also access the Write Checks screen by pressing Ctrl-W from the QuickBooks Main menu.

Writing a Check

To write a check, follow these steps:

1. Press Ctrl-W from the Main menu to access the Write Checks screen. Look in the bottom left corner of this screen to make sure the account you are working in (the current account) is the checking account you use to write checks. (See Lesson 21 to learn how to select your checking account if it is not the current account.)

2. QuickBooks fills in the current date in the Date field. To enter a different date, press Shift-Tab to position the cursor in the Date field, type a new date, and press Enter.

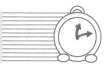

    Changing Dates To change the date quickly in the Write Checks screen's Date field, press + to increase the date one day at a time, or press – to decrease the date one day at a time.

3. Type the payee's name in the Pay to the Order of field, and press Enter. If the payee is listed in the Customer, Vendor, or Employee List, press Ctrl-L to display the Payee List (see Lesson 6), and select the payee from the list.

4. In the Amount field, type the check amount; separate dollars and cents with a decimal (maximum amount: $9,999,999.99). Press Enter. QuickBooks enters the written dollar amount on the next line automatically.

5. If you are using window envelopes to mail your checks, you may type up to four lines in the Address field if QuickBooks did not complete it.

6. If you have turned on the company option that controls the extra message line on checks (see Lesson 24), QuickBooks provides a (Msg) field that lets you enter a message (up to 24 characters) on your check. Press Enter after you type your message.

7. Press Tab to move to the Memo field. If desired, type a memo and press Enter.

8. The next section of the check is the Voucher, where you assign account, subaccounts, and projects to a check transaction. Type the account you want to assign to the check transaction in the Account field, and press Enter.

Assigning Accounts to Check Transactions You can assign an account to a check transaction directly from the Chart of Accounts by pressing Ctrl-L to display the Chart of Accounts. Then use the Up and Down arrow keys to move the arrow to the account you want to assign to the transaction; press Enter to fill in the Account field with this account's name.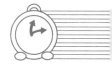

Transfer Transactions To record a transfer from your checking account to another account (say, your savings account), enter the name of the savings account in the Account field. QuickBooks enters the account name, enclosed in brackets to show that the transaction is a transfer from one QuickBooks account (checking) to another account (savings). Lesson 9 explains more about transfer transactions.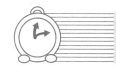

9. If you want to assign a project to the check transaction (optional), press Ctrl-L from the Project field to display the Projects List. Select a project from the list and

press Enter. Note that QuickBooks does not display the Project field unless you set the company option that activates project tracking (see Lesson 24).

10. At the Description field, type a description or memo (using up to 27 characters), and press Enter.

Assigning More than One Account to a Check Transaction   You can assign more than one account to a transaction. This is called *splitting the transaction*. Splitting transactions allows you to classify your checks accurately by assigning more than one account to transactions that include more than one type of expense. See Lesson 10 to learn how to split transactions.

11. Press Ctrl-Enter or F10 to record the check.

Reviewing and Editing Checks

Before you print a check, you should review (and edit if necessary) the check to ensure that there are no errors. You can review and edit checks in the Check Register or at the Write Checks screen. To review and edit a check at the Write Checks screen, follow these steps:

1. Access the Write Checks screen by pressing Ctrl-W from the Main menu.

2. Use the following keys to scroll through the checks at the Write Checks screen and display the check that you want to edit:

Ctrl-PgUp to display the preceding check.

Ctrl-PgDn to display the next check.

Ctrl-Home or Home Home Home to display the first check.

Ctrl-End or End End End to display the last check (a blank check).

3. Review the check, and make any necessary changes by typing over the entries in the Write Checks screen. Use the following keys to help you move around the Write Checks screen:

Enter or Tab to move forward one field.

Shift-Tab to move backward one field.

Home to move to the beginning of the current field.

Home Home to move to the beginning of the first field in the current check.

End to move to the end of the current field.

End End to move to the last field in the current check.

Ctrl-Right arrow to move forward one word within a field.

Ctrl-Left arrow to move backward one word within a field.

Ctrl-S to move to the voucher.

PgUp to move up within the voucher.

PgDn to move down within the voucher.

Shift-Enter to move to the Date, Memo, or Accounts fields.

4. Press Ctrl-Enter or F10 to record the changes, or Esc to cancel the changes.

5. QuickBooks displays the next check automatically.

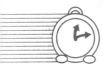

Finding Checks   You can use the Find (Ctrl-F) and Go to Date features of QuickBooks to locate a check. (See Lesson 9.)

Deleting a Check

Checks you have written but have not printed can be deleted at any time, from either the Write Checks screen or the Check Register. To delete a check from the Write Checks screen, follow these steps:

1. Access the Write Checks screen by pressing Ctrl-W from the Main menu.

2. Use the Ctrl-PgUp, Ctrl-PgDn, Ctrl-Home, or Ctrl-End keys to display the check you want to delete.

3. Press F3 to access the Find/Edit menu shown in Figure 7.2.

4. Select Delete Check from the Find/Edit menu (or press Ctrl-D).

5. QuickBooks displays the OK to Delete Transaction? window. Press Enter or 1 to delete the check.

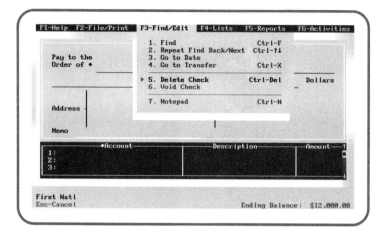

Figure 7.2   Access the Find/Edit menu to delete a check.

Voiding a Check

You can *void* (cancel) a check you have written and printed using QuickBooks. Checks are voided in the Check Register. (When you select the Void Check option from the Write Checks screen, QuickBooks moves to the Check Register). See Lesson 9 to learn how to void a check in the Check Register.

In the next lesson, you will learn how to print checks.

Lesson 8
Printing Checks

In this lesson, you will learn how to print checks using QuickBooks.

Ordering Checks

If you plan to use QuickBooks to print checks, you should order preprinted checks from Intuit, publisher of QuickBooks. Intuit offers checks to fit continuous-feed printers and single-sheet (such as laser and inkjet) printers. Sample checks are included in your QuickBooks package; review them to determine which type works best for your small business.

To order checks, complete the order form included in your QuickBooks package, or print an order form from the QuickBooks program by following these steps:

1. Press Ctrl-W from the Main menu to access the Write Checks screen.

2. Press F2 to display the File/Print pull-down menu.

3. Select the Print Supplies Order Form option. QuickBooks displays the Print Supplies Order Form window.

4. If your printer appears in the `Print to` field, press Ctrl-Enter or F10 to print the order form. If your printer does not appear in the `Print to` field, press Ctrl-L to display the list of printers, and then select your printer from the list.

Positioning Checks in Your Printer

You need to align your QuickBooks checks in your printer before you start printing. Aligning checks in your continuous-feed printer is easy with QuickBooks' automatic alignment feature.

Aligning Continuous-Feed Checks in Your Printer

To align continuous-feed checks in your printer, follow these steps:

1. Insert the sample checks into your printer (as you would continuous-feed paper) and turn on your printer.

2. Press Ctrl-W from the Main menu to access the Write Checks screen. Make sure that you have at least one check to print. If not, complete and record a test check (you can delete it later).

3. Press F2 to display the File/Print pull-down menu.

4. Select the Print Checks option (or press Ctrl-P).

5. QuickBooks displays the Print Checks window shown in Figure 8.1.

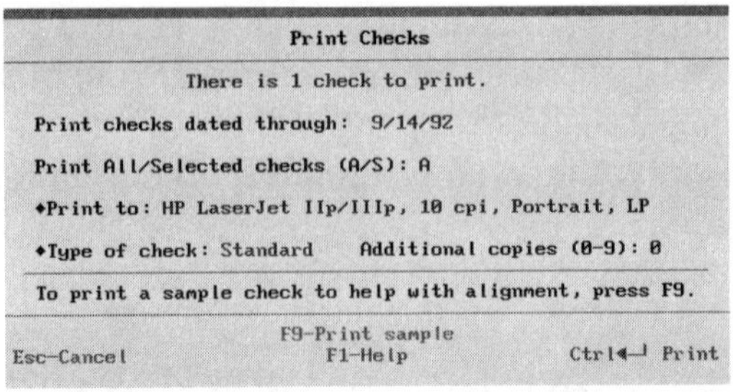

```
                        Print Checks
                  There is 1 check to print.
        Print checks dated through:  9/14/92

        Print All/Selected checks (A/S): A

        ◆Print to: HP LaserJet IIp/IIIp, 10 cpi, Portrait, LP

        ◆Type of check: Standard     Additional copies (0-9): 0

        To print a sample check to help with alignment, press F9.

                          F9-Print sample
        Esc-Cancel            F1-Help             Ctrl◄┘ Print
```

Figure 8.1   The Print Checks window.

6. If your printer does not appear in the Print to field (or if you want to select a different printer), press Tab twice to move to the Print to field, and press Ctrl-L to display the printer list. Choose a printer from the list, and press Enter.

7. At the Type of check field, press Ctrl-L to display the list of available check types. Select a type of check to test, and press Enter.

8. Press F9 and then press Enter at the message that follows. Do not adjust your printer now.

9. QuickBooks prints the sample check and displays the Automatic Form Alignment window (shown in Figure 8.2).

10. Review the sample check without moving the checks in your printer. If the sample check printed correctly, go to step 12. If the vertical alignment of the sample check is incorrect, type the position number of the Pointer Line (the horizontal line printed on the sample check) in the Position number field, and press Enter to print a second sample check.

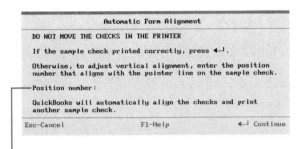

Type the position number of the Pointer Line to adjust the checks properly in your printer.

Figure 8.2 Use the Automatic Form Alignment window to adjust the alignment of continuous-feed checks.

11. Review the second sample check. If the sample check printed correctly, proceed to the next step. Otherwise, use the knob on the side of your printer which turns the paper roller to adjust the check, and repeat step 10.

12. When the alignment of the checks is correct, press Enter at the Automatic Form Alignment window to return to the Print Checks window.

Printing a Sample Laser Check

To print a sample laser check, follow these steps:

1. Insert blank checks in your laser printer (the same way you insert letterhead paper) and turn on your printer.

2. Press Ctrl-W from the Main menu to access the Write Checks screen. Make sure you have at least one check to print. If not, complete and record a test check (you can delete it later).

3. Press F2 to display the File/Print pull-down menu.

4. Select the Print Checks option (or press Ctrl-P).

5. QuickBooks displays the Print Checks window shown in Figure 8.1.

6. If your laser printer does not appear in the Print to field (or if you want to select a different printer), press Tab twice to move to the Print to field, and press Ctrl-L to display the printer list. Choose a printer from the list, and press Enter.

7. At the Type of check field, press Ctrl-L to display the list of available check types. Select a type of check to test, and press Enter.

8. Press F9 to print the sample laser check.

9. Review the sample check. If the sample check did not print correctly, refer to the "Common Printing Problems and Solutions" section of your QuickBooks manual.

Printing Checks

When your checks are properly positioned in your printer, you're ready to print checks. To print checks using QuickBooks, follow these steps:

1. Turn on your printer and make sure that it is on-line.

2. Press Ctrl-W from the Main menu to access the Write Checks screen.

3. Press F2 to display the File/Print pull-down menu and select the Print Checks option (or press Ctrl-P).

4. QuickBooks displays the Print Checks window (shown in Figure 8.1), tells you how many checks you have to print, and shows the number of postdated checks (if any).

Postdated Checks   Checks written with a future date. Postdated checks can be printed at any time.

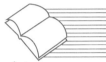

5. At the `Print checks dated through` field, type the date through which you want checks printed, and press Enter. QuickBooks prints only those checks dated on or before this date.

6. At the `Print All/Selected checks` field, type `s` to select which checks to print; otherwise, press Enter (which leaves the setting at `A` and prints all checks).

7. If the printer you are using does not appear in the `Print to` field, press Ctrl-L to display the printer list, select the appropriate printer from the list, and press Enter.

8. At the `Type of check` field, press Ctrl-L to display the available check types, select the type of check you are printing, and press Enter.

9. If you're using multipart laser checks, press Tab to move to the `Additional copies` field, and type the additional number of copies to print.

10. Press Ctrl-Enter or F10. If you typed `s` in the Print All/ Selected checks field, QuickBooks displays the Select Checks to Print window. See the next section to learn how to select checks to print.

11. QuickBooks displays the Set Check Number window, shown in Figure 8.3.

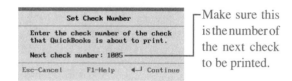

Make sure this is the number of the next check to be printed.

Figure 8.3 Use the Set Check Number window to assign the next check number to the first printed check.

12. If the check number shown is not correct, type the number of the next blank check. When the Set Check Number window shows the correct check number, press Enter to begin printing checks. If you're printing on a partial page of checks, see the section "Printing on a Partial Page" later in this lesson.

Changing Check Numbers Use the + and − keys to increase or decrease the check number by one number at a time.

Duplicate Check Numbers If you assign a duplicate check number (one you've already used) to a check transaction, QuickBooks shows you the information for the check you assigned that number, using a window labeled Warning: Duplicate Number. Press Y to print the check with the duplicate check number, or N to go back to the Set Check Number window and change the check number. If you don't want to be warned of duplicate check numbers, you can turn off the company option that controls the duplicate check warning. (Refer to Lesson 24 to learn how to turn off company options.)

Preventing Unauthorized Check Printing You can prevent unauthorized persons from printing checks by using passwords. Assigning a password to the check printing activity is explained in Lesson 24.

Selecting Checks to Print

If you don't want to print all checks through the specified date, you can select specific checks to print. To select checks to print, follow these steps:

1. At the Print Checks window (shown in Figure 8.1), press S in the `Print All/Selected checks` field.

2. After all other fields in the Print Checks window are filled in, press Ctrl-Enter or F10.

3. QuickBooks displays the Select Checks to Print window shown in Figure 8.4. All Checks in the Select Checks to Print window are marked to print.

4. Move the arrow to a check you don't want to print, and press Spacebar to deselect it. Repeat these steps for each check you do not want to print.

5. Press Ctrl-Enter or F10 to go to the Set Check Number window.

6. Follow steps 11 and 12 in the preceding section on printing checks.

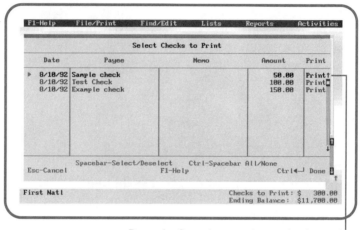

Press the Spacebar to select a check to print.

Figure 8.4   Use the Select Checks to Print window to select the checks you want to print.

Printing on a Partial Page of Checks   Leave the half-inch strip attached to the bottom of the page, and complete the Print Checks window (as explained earlier in this lesson). Press Ctrl-Enter or F10, and enter the next blank check number. Then press F9 and type the number of checks remaining on the page and the printing mode. Press Enter, and then press Ctrl-Enter to begin printing.

Reprinting Checks   To reprint a check, access the Check Register (see Lesson 9) and highlight the transaction for the check. Then type an asterisk (*) over the existing check number in the Num field. Press Ctrl-Enter or F10 to record the change and go to the Write Checks screen to print the check as usual.

In the next lesson, you will learn how to enter transactions in the Check Register.

Lesson 9

Using the Check Register

In this lesson, you will learn how to use the Check Register to record all activity that affects your checking account balance.

Working with the Check Register

The QuickBooks *Check Register* is similar to a manual Check Register in the way it records all checking account activity.

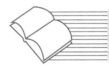

Check Register   A Check Register pertains specifically to a checking or other type of bank account. For each transaction, the Check Register lists the date of the transaction, the check number, payee or deposit source, payment amount or deposit amount, memo message (optional), account assigned to the transaction, status of the transaction (whether it has cleared the banks), and the remaining balance in the account.

If you write checks using QuickBooks, your transactions are recorded automatically in the Check Register. Deposits, ATM withdrawals, adjustments, bank service charges, and interest earned are entered directly into the Check Register. QuickBooks adjusts your checking account balance for each transaction entered.

Accessing the Check Register

To access the Check Register, follow these steps:

1. From the QuickBooks Main menu, select the Checkbook option.

2. From the Checkbook menu, choose the Check Register option.

3. QuickBooks displays the Check Register shown in Figure 9.1.

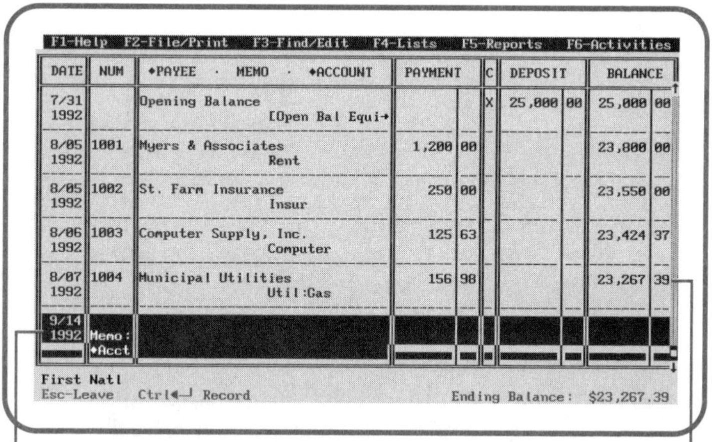

Enter new transactions in the highlighted area.

Calculated account balance after a transaction.

Figure 9.1 The Check Register.

Quick Access   Press Ctrl-R from the Write Checks screen to access the Check Register quickly.

Entering Transactions in the Check Register

To enter transactions in the blank transaction line at the end of the Check Register, follow these steps:

1. Access the Check Register, as explained above.

2. Press Ctrl-End to highlight the next empty transaction line.

3. QuickBooks enters the current date in the Date field. Press + or – to increase or decrease the date one day at a time. Press Enter.

4. In the Num field, type the number of the manual check you are writing. If you are entering a deposit, enter the deposit number. If you are entering an automatic teller machine transaction, type ATM. Press Enter.

5. In the Payee field, type the payee's name or press Ctrl-L to display the Payee List and select a payee from the list. Press Enter.

6. Type check amounts, bank charges, or other checking account fees in the Payment field. Type deposit amounts (or any other increases in your checking account) in the Deposit field. Press Enter.

7. Type a memo, if desired, and press Enter.

8. At the Account field, type the name of the account you want to assign to the transaction, and press Enter. (Press Ctrl-L to select an account from the Chart of Accounts.) If you want to record a transfer from your checking account to another balance sheet account, enter that other account's name in the Account field. (You learn more about transfer transactions later in this lesson.) If you want to assign more than one account or subaccount to a transaction, you can split the transaction (as explained in Lesson 10).

9. If you want to assign a project to the transactions (optional), type a project name in the Project field (or press Ctrl-L to display the list of projects, and select one from the list). See Lesson 6 for more on the Project List.

10. Press Ctrl-Enter or F10 to record the transaction in the Check Register.

Entering a Transfer Transaction

Most transactions you enter will affect one balance sheet account, your checking account, and another income or expense account. For example, when you write a check for office supplies, rent, or insurance, you assign expense accounts to the transactions in your checking account. You can also record transactions in QuickBooks that affect more than one account, as when you transfer money from one balance sheet account (the *source account*) to another (the *destination account*). If you transfer money from your checking account to your savings account, for example, the transfer has changed two balance sheet accounts: it decreases the balance in checking and increases the balance in savings. You don't have to enter two transactions, however, when transferring funds—just enter a transfer transaction in the source account. QuickBooks enters a parallel transaction in the destination account automatically.

To enter a transfer transaction in the Check Register, follow these steps:

1. Access the Check Register, as explained earlier in this lesson.

2. Enter the transaction information as usual, except for the account.

3. At the Account field, press Ctrl-L to display the Chart Of Accounts list.

4. Select a balance sheet account and press Enter. QuickBooks enters the name of the selected account, enclosed in brackets to indicate a transfer transaction.

5. Press Ctrl-Enter or F10 to record the transfer transaction.

Finding Transfer Transactions   To quickly find the corresponding transfer transaction in the destination account, highlight the transfer transaction in the source account register, and press Ctrl-X. QuickBooks accesses the proper register and highlights the corresponding transfer transaction.

Finding Transactions in the Check Register

To quickly find a transaction without scrolling through the entire Check Register, follow these steps:

1. From the Check Register, press F3 to access the Find/ Edit pull-down menu.

2. Select the Find option from the Find/Edit menu (or press Ctrl-F).

3. QuickBooks displays the Transaction to Find window (shown in Figure 9.2).

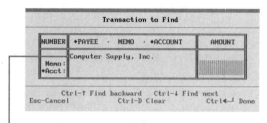

Enter information to help QuickBooks find a transaction in the system.

Figure 9.2 Use the Transaction to Find window to enter information about the transaction you want to find.

4. Type the information that matches the transaction for which you are searching. You can ask QuickBooks to find transactions that match payment or deposit amounts, payees, memos, accounts, or projects. Press Ctrl-D to clear the Transaction to Find window.

5. Press Ctrl-Up arrow to search backwards, or Ctrl-Down arrow to search forward. Continue pressing Ctrl-Up arrow or Ctrl-Down arrow until you have found the transaction for which you are looking.

Key Word Matches   If you are unsure of the exact words or phrases used in the transaction you are trying to find, enter double periods (..) before or after a key word. For example, if you know that the name of a payee contains the word "Computer," type `computer..` and QuickBooks will find transactions that begin with the word *computer* (such as Computer Superstore, Computer Supplies, or Computer Graphics).

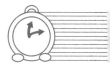

Moving to a Specific Date

To find transactions in the Check Register that occurred on a specific date, follow these steps:

1. From the Check Register, press F3 to access the Find/ Edit pull-down menu.

2. Select the Go to Date option. QuickBooks displays the Go to Date window.

3. Type the date or press the + or – keys to change the date one day at a time.

4. Press Enter. QuickBooks finds the first transaction with the date you entered in the Go to Date window.

Editing a Transaction in the Check Register

You can make changes to a transaction you have entered in the Check Register. You cannot, however, edit or change the amount calculated in the Balance column of the Check Register. To edit a transaction, follow these steps:

1. Access the Check Register, as explained earlier in this lesson.

2. Use the following keys to move quickly through the Check Register to highlight the transaction you want to edit:

   Up arrow to move up one transaction line.

   Down arrow to move down one transaction line.

   PgUp to move up one screen of transactions.

   PgDn to move down one screen of transactions.

   Ctrl-PgUp to move to the beginning of the preceding month.

   Ctrl-PgDn to move to the beginning of the next month.

   Ctrl-Home to move to the beginning of the Check Register.

   Ctrl-End to move to the end of the Check Register (the blank transaction line).

3. Make the necessary changes to the transaction.

4. Press Ctrl-Enter or F10 to record the edited transaction.

Canceling Changes   If you want to cancel the changes made to a transaction, press Esc before recording the transaction. QuickBooks displays the Leaving Transaction window, where you press 2 to cancel the changes made to the transaction and leave the Check Register.

Deleting a Transaction in the Check Register

If you inadvertently entered a transaction twice, entered it in the wrong register, or made another such error, you can delete the transaction from the Check Register. This process removes the transaction's information from the Check Register permanently. You should *void* transactions for checks you have written and printed, however, so you have complete records of all your check numbers.

To delete a transaction from the Check Register, follow these steps:

1. In the Check Register, highlight the transaction you want to delete.

2. Press F3 to access the Find/Edit pull-down menu, and select the Delete Transaction option (or press Ctrl-Del).

3. QuickBooks displays the OK to Delete Transaction? window. Press Enter or 1 to delete the transaction.

Voiding a Check in the Check Register

You may need to void a check when you want to stop payment, when you lose a check and write another one to replace it, or when a check prints incorrectly and you have to print another. When you *void* a check, QuickBooks retains the transaction line with the check number in the Check Register, but erases the amount of the check and adjusts the checking account balance accordingly.

To void a check in the Check Register, follow these steps:

1. Use the keys listed in the "Editing a Transaction" section of this lesson to highlight the transaction for the check you want to void.

2. Press F3 to access the Find/Edit pull-down menu, and select the Void Transaction option.

3. QuickBooks enters the word VOID in the Payee field, and marks the transaction with an X in the Clear column .

Printing the Check Register   You can print the Check Register by pressing Ctrl-P and entering the period you want to include in the printed register. You can specify whether to print one transaction per line, split transaction detail, or sort the report by check number or date.

In the next lesson, you will learn how to assign more than one account to a transaction by splitting the transaction.

Lesson 10
Working with Split Transactions

In this lesson, you will learn how to assign more than one account to a transaction by splitting the transaction.

Splitting Transactions

You can assign more than one account to a transaction by *splitting the transaction*. For example, if you write a check for office supplies, computer supplies, and business forms, you must assign three different accounts to the check transaction so the transaction is properly allocated to each expense. You can split transactions at the Write Checks screen when writing a check, or at the Check Register when entering a transaction for a manual check. QuickBooks allows you to assign up to 31 accounts to a single transaction.

To split a transaction, follow these steps:

1. Access the Check Register.

2. Enter all transaction information and the amount of the transaction as usual.

3. Move to the Account field and press F3 to access the Find/Edit pull-down menu.

4. Select the Split Transaction option from the Find/Edit menu (or press Ctrl-S). QuickBooks displays the Split Transaction window shown in Figure 10.1.

```
                        Split Transaction
              *Account                Description          Amount
  1:Computer                   computer supplies          125.58
  2:Supplies:Office            stationery                  95.26
  3:Printing                   printed ads                 35.55
  4:
  5:
  6:
  7:
  Esc-Cancel    Ctrl-D Delete line   F9-Recalc transaction total  Ctrl◄─┘ Done
```

One transaction has been split among three accounts.

Amounts in the Split Transaction window equal the transaction amount in the register.

Figure 10.1 Use the Split Transaction window to assign more than one account to a transaction.

5. Position the cursor in the Account field in line 1, and press Ctrl-L to select an account from the Chart Of Accounts list.

6. Move to the Project field in line 1 (if displayed) and press Ctrl-L to select a project. (Note that assigning projects is optional.)

7. In the Description field in line 1, type a description for the first account, and press Enter.

8. In the Amount field, type the amount to be allocated to the first account, and press Enter. (Note that you can enter positive or negative amounts in the Amount field.)

9. Move to line 2 in the Split Transaction window, and repeat steps 5 through 8.

10. Continue entering lines in the Split Transaction window until the total amount of the transaction has been allocated to accounts.

11. Press Ctrl-Enter or F10 to return to the transaction in the Check Register.

12. Press Ctrl-Enter or F10 to record the split transaction. QuickBooks enters the word SPLIT in the Num field of a split transaction.

Splitting Transactions at the Write Checks Screen   The procedures you follow to split a transaction at the Write Checks screen are the same as those for splitting a transaction in the Check Register, except you don't enter accounts at the Split Transaction window. Instead, enter accounts in the Voucher part of the Write Checks screen (which includes 31 lines). To move quickly to the Voucher area of the Write Checks screen, press Ctrl-S.

Calculating Split Transactions   As you enter each line of a split transaction, QuickBooks calculates the remaining balance of the transaction, and enters the result in the next account line.

Copying in the Split Transaction Window   To copy the contents of the preceding line in the Split Transaction window, type " in the Account field on the next line, and press Enter.

Splitting Transactions by Percentages

You can allocate percentages to split transactions. For example, you may want to allocate an expense between business and personal use, 75% business and 25% personal. To split transactions by percentages, follow these steps:

1. Follow the steps just explained to open the Split Transaction window.

2. Enter the account, project (if desired), and description as usual.

3. In the Amount field, type the percentage that you want allocated to the first account. Percentages are entered as xx% (for example, enter seventy-five percent as 75%).

4. Press Enter and QuickBooks multiplies the transaction amount by the percentage, and enters the result in the Amount field.

5. Repeat steps 2 through 4 to split the transaction further.

Editing Split Transactions

You can change the information in a split transaction. To edit a split transaction, follow these steps:

1. In the Check Register, highlight the split transaction you want to edit.

2. Press Ctrl-S to access the Split Transaction window.

3. Make any necessary changes to the Split Transaction window.

4. Press Ctrl-Enter or F10 to return to the transaction in the Check Register.

5. Press Ctrl-Enter or F10 to record the changes to the split transaction.

Deleting Lines in a Split Transaction

To delete a line in a split transaction, follow these steps:

1. In the Check Register, highlight the split transaction from which you want to delete a line.

2. Press Ctrl-S to access the Split Transaction window.

3. In the Split Transaction window, move to the line you want to delete and press Ctrl-D.

Deleting Entire Split Transactions   To delete an entire split transaction, highlight it in the Check Register and press Ctrl-D. At the OK to Delete Transaction? window, press Enter or 1 to delete.

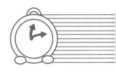

Undoing Split Transactions

If you want to undo a split transaction so that the transaction is assigned to only one account, follow these steps:

1. In the Check Register, highlight the split transaction you want to undo.

2. Press Ctrl-S to access the Split Transaction window.

3. Delete each line in the Split Transaction window by positioning the cursor on each line and pressing Ctrl-D.

4. When all lines in the Split Transaction window are deleted, press Esc to return to the transaction in the Check Register.

5. Enter one account in the Account field, and press Ctrl-Enter or F10 to record the transaction.

Recalculating Split Transaction Amounts As you are entering lines in the Split Transaction window, you can recalculate the transaction amount by pressing F9. When you do so, QuickBooks totals the amounts in the Split Transaction window, and enters that amount in the Check Register's Payment or Deposit field, or in the Write Checks screen's Amount field.

In the next lesson, you will learn how to memorize transactions so you can enter recurring transactions in QuickBooks with greater speed and accuracy.

Lesson 11
Working with Memorized Transactions

In this lesson, you will learn how to have QuickBooks memorize and recall transactions.

Using Memorized Transactions

You can record your transactions quickly in the Check Register, the Write Checks screen, or any other account register by using QuickBooks to *memorize* the transaction and *recall* it later.

To *memorize* a transaction is to save information from it to be recalled for later transactions. If you memorize and recall frequently-recorded transactions (such as rent payments, insurance premiums, or loan payments), you won't have to enter unchanging information about them over and over. You can memorize any type of transaction you enter in the Check Register and Write Check screen—including checks, deposits, bank charges, and automatic teller transactions.

Note that you can memorize invoice transactions at the Write Invoice screen or the Accounts Receivable register. (See Lesson 14 to learn about memorizing invoices.)

Memorizing a Transaction

To memorize a transaction in the Check Register, follow these steps:

1. In the Check Register, enter the transaction you want to memorize (as little or as much of it as you want).

2. With the transaction highlighted, press F4 to access the Lists pull-down menu.

3. Select the Memorize Transaction option from the Lists menu (or press Ctrl-M).

4. QuickBooks displays a message telling you it will memorize the highlighted fields. Press Enter to memorize them.

5. QuickBooks returns to the Check Register. Complete the transaction, if necessary, and press Ctrl-Enter or F10 if you want to record the transaction entered in step 1.

Memorizing Recorded Transactions   You can memorize transactions that have already been recorded in the Check Register. Just highlight the transaction you want to memorize, and press Ctrl-M. QuickBooks memorizes the entire transaction, except date and check number.

Memorizing Checks To memorize checks at the Write Checks screen, follow the same steps as for memorizing transactions in the Check Register. Display the check you want to memorize, and press Ctrl-M.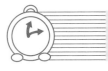

Recalling a Memorized Transaction

Once you have memorized a transaction, you can recall the transaction and record it in the Check Register or the Write Checks screen.

To recall a memorized transaction in the Check Register, follow these steps:

1. At the Check Register, press Ctrl-End to highlight the blank transaction line at the end of the register.

Overwriting Existing Transactions If you recall a memorized transaction into a transaction line with a recorded transaction, QuickBooks overwrites the existing information with the memorized information.

2. Press F4 to access the Lists pull-down menu, and select the Recall Transaction option (or press Ctrl-T).

3. QuickBooks displays the Standard Memorized Transaction List shown in Figure 11.1.

Memorized transaction

Type column indicates a payment, deposit, or check.

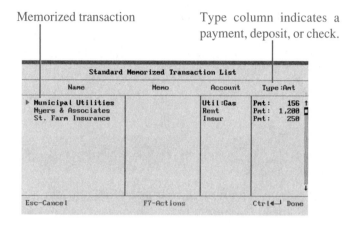

Figure 11.1 The Standard Memorized Transaction List that includes all memorized transactions.

4. Move the arrow to the memorized transaction you want to recall, and press Enter.

5. QuickBooks enters the memorized transaction information into the Check Register. Make any necessary changes to the transaction.

6. Press Ctrl-Enter or F10 to record the recalled transaction.

Recalling Memorized Checks To recall memorized checks at the Write Checks screen, display a blank check and press Ctrl-T to display the Standard Memorized Transaction List. Then select the memorized check you want to recall, and press Enter.

Editing a Memorized Transaction

To change a memorized transaction, first recall it, and then make the changes in the Check Register or the Write Checks screen. To edit a memorized transaction in the Check Register:

1. At the Check Register, press Ctrl-End to highlight the blank transaction line at the end of the register.

2. Press Ctrl-T to display the Standard Memorized Transaction List; select the memorized transaction you want to edit. Press Enter.

3. QuickBooks enters the memorized transaction into the Check Register. Now you can make any necessary changes to it.

4. Press Ctrl-M to memorize the edited transaction. QuickBooks highlights the information it is about to memorize from the transaction. Press Enter.

5. QuickBooks next asks whether you want to replace the original memorized transaction with the changed transaction. Press 1 to make this replacement, or press 2 to add the changed transaction to the Standard Memorized Transaction List instead.

Deleting a Memorized Transaction

At any time, you can delete a memorized transaction from the Standard Memorized Transaction List. To delete a memorized transaction, follow these steps:

1. From the Check Register or the Write Checks screen, press Ctrl-T to display the Standard Memorized Transaction List shown in Figure 11.1.

2. Move the arrow to the memorized transaction you want to delete.

3. Press F7 to access the Actions menu, and select the Delete option (or press Ctrl-D).

4. QuickBooks warns that you are about to delete a memorized transaction permanently. Press Enter to delete it.

In the next lesson, you will learn how to use transaction groups to gain fast access to groups of transactions that occur at the same intervals.

Lesson 12

Grouping Transactions

In this lesson, you will learn how to set up and execute transaction groups.

Setting Up Transaction Groups

Transaction groups can have just one transaction or many. For example, you may want to set up a transaction group for bills due at the same time each month (such as your rent, loan payments, and insurance premiums).

Transaction Group   A group of recurring transactions that you pay or add to your account at the same time.

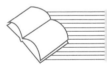

To set up a transaction group, follow these steps:

1. Memorize the transactions you want to include in the transaction group (see Lesson 11).

2. From an account register or the Write Checks screen, select Transaction Group from the Lists menu or press Ctrl-J.

3. QuickBooks displays the Standard Transaction Group List. Press F7 to display the Actions menu, and select the Add New option (or press Ctrl-Ins).

4. QuickBooks displays the Add New Standard Transaction Group window shown in Figure 12.1.

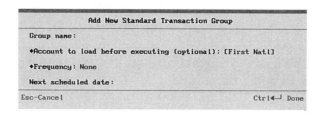

```
                    Add New Standard Transaction Group

Group name:

◆Account to load before executing (optional): [First Nat'l]

◆Frequency: None

Next scheduled date:

Esc-Cancel                                          Ctrl↵ Done
```

Figure 12.1   Use the Add New Standard Transaction Group window to set up a transaction group.

5. In the Group name field, type a name for the transaction group using up to 20 characters. Press Enter.

6. In the Account to load field, press Ctrl-L to display a list of accounts; choose the account in which you want QuickBooks to enter transactions. (By default, QuickBooks chooses your checking account.) Press Enter.

7. Press Ctrl-L at the Frequency field to display a list of options, from which you select how often the transaction group is due (weekly, every two weeks, monthly, quarterly, and so forth). Press Enter.

8. In the Next scheduled date field, type the next date the transaction group is due. Press Enter.

9. Press Ctrl-Enter.

10. QuickBooks displays the Standard Memorized Transaction List. Move the arrow to each transaction you want to include in the transaction group. Press the Spacebar to include the transaction. To unassign a transaction to a group, press the Spacebar again.

11. When you finish selecting transactions, press Ctrl-Enter to set up the transaction group.

Adding and Deleting Transactions in a Transaction Group

You can add or delete transactions from the group at any time. To add or delete a transaction, follow these steps:

1. From an account register or the Write Checks screen, select Transaction Group from the Lists menu or press Ctrl-J.

2. QuickBooks displays the Standard Transaction Group List shown in Figure 12.2.

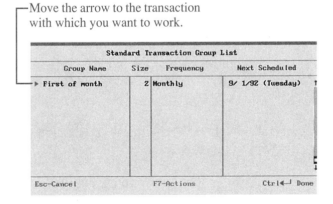

Figure 12.2   The Standard Transaction Group List.

3. Move the arrow to the transaction group to which you want to add a transaction or from which you want to delete a transaction.

4. Press F7 to access the Actions menu, and select the View/Edit option or just press Ctrl-E.

5. Press Ctrl-Enter to go to the Standard Memorized Transaction List.

6. Move the arrow to the memorized transaction you want to include in the transaction group. Press the Spacebar to include the transaction. To delete a transaction, move the arrow to the memorized transaction you want to delete; press the Spacebar to remove the word Include from the transaction.

7. Press Ctrl-Enter.

Editing a Transaction Group

You can change the description, the account in which QuickBooks enters a transaction, the frequency, or the next scheduled date for a transaction group. To edit a transaction group, follow these steps:

1. From an account register or the Write Checks screen, select Transaction Group from the Lists menu or press Ctrl-J.

2. QuickBooks displays the Standard Transaction Group List shown in Figure 12.2.

3. Move the arrow to the transaction group you want to edit.

4. Press Ctrl-E to select the View/Edit option.

5. QuickBooks displays the View/Edit Standard Transaction Group window. Move to the field you want to change, and type over the existing information.

6. Press Ctrl-Enter to go to the Standard Memorized Transaction List.

7. Press the Spacebar to assign or unassign any transactions to the group.

8. Press Ctrl-Enter to save the changes to the transaction group.

Deleting a Transaction Group

To delete a transaction group, follow these steps:

1. From an account register or the Write Checks screen, select Transaction Group from the Lists menu or press Ctrl-J.

2. QuickBooks displays the Standard Transaction Group List shown in Figure 12.2.

3. Move the arrow to the transaction group you want to delete.

4. Press Ctrl-Del to select the Delete option.

5. QuickBooks warns you that you are about to delete a transaction group permanently.

6. Press Enter to delete the transaction group.

Executing a Transaction Group

When you *execute* a transaction group, QuickBooks records each of the group's transactions in the Account register. Then you can make any changes to these transactions from the register. To execute a transaction group, follow these steps:

1. From an account register or the Write Checks screen, select Transaction Group from the Lists menu or press Ctrl-J.

2. Move the arrow to the transaction group you want to execute.

3. Press Enter to display the Transaction Group Date window shown in Figure 12.3.

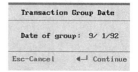

Figure 12.3   The Transaction Group Date window, showing the date given to transactions when they are recorded in the register.

4. Use the + or – keys to change the date if needed.

5. Press Enter to execute the transaction group. QuickBooks enters and records the transactions in the Account register and highlights the first transaction so that you can make any necessary changes to it or the following transactions.

Lesson 13

Reconciling Your Checking Account

In this lesson, you will learn how to reconcile your checking account using QuickBooks.

Why Reconcile Your Account?

A bank reconciliation is a procedure that compares the balance shown on your bank statement at the end of a specific period to the balance shown in the Check Register at the end of the same period. You should reconcile your account with your bank statement each time you receive a statement to ensure:

- You recorded the same transactions the bank statement shows.

- Your recorded transactions are accurate.

- The bank statement reflects your transactions correctly for the period. (Banks sometimes make mistakes!)

Entering Information from Your Bank Statement

To begin reconciling your account, you must enter the information on your bank statement in QuickBooks. To enter information from your bank statement, follow these steps:

1. Access the Check Register or the Write Checks screen. Make sure that the current account (displayed in the lower left corner of the screen) is the checking account or bank account you are reconciling. If not, press Ctrl-A to select the appropriate account from the Chart Of Accounts list.

2. Press F6 to access the Activities menu and select the Reconcile option (or press Ctrl-Y).

3. QuickBooks displays the Reconcile Register with Bank Statement window, as shown in Figure 13.1.

Enter your statement amounts.

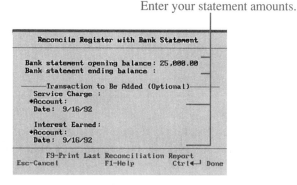

Figure 13.1 The Reconcile Register with Bank Statement window to enter information from your bank statement.

4. Compare the opening balance shown in the window with the opening balance shown on your statement. If this is the first time you have reconciled your account with QuickBooks, there may be a difference in the Bank statement opening balance field. If necessary, type the correct opening balance, and press Enter.

5. Type the ending balance shown on your bank statement, and press Enter.

6. Type any transactions to be added: service charges and interest earned, and an account name to assign to the transactions. Also, type the dates these transactions occurred. (Note: If you want to print your last reconciliation report, press F9 from the Reconcile Register with Bank Statement window.)

7. Press Ctrl-Enter to record the information in the Reconcile Register with Bank Statement window and continue with the reconciliation. If there was no opening balance difference, QuickBooks displays a list of uncleared transactions and you can proceed to the section "Marking Cleared Transactions" in this lesson. If there was an opening balance difference, proceed to the next section ("Adjusting Opening Balance Differences").

Leaving the Reconciliation   If you need to leave the reconciliation process before it is complete, just press Esc. Then press 2 to leave the reconciliation, save your work, and return to the Check Register or the Write Checks screen.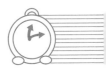

Adjusting Opening Balance Differences

If you changed the amount in the Bank Statement opening balance field (in the Reconcile Register with Bank Statement window), QuickBooks displays a message that the opening balance does not match the bank's. The difference may be due to the following reasons:

- You're reconciling for the first time, and QuickBooks is using the opening balance you entered when you set up your checking account.

- You entered previous transactions before you began using QuickBooks but did not mark the transactions as cleared.

- You are not using the most current bank statement.

Press Enter at the message screen to continue with the reconciliation. Note that you will have to resolve the opening balance difference later in the reconciliation process. (See "Adjusting for Differences" later in this lesson.)

Marking Cleared Transactions

The next step in reconciling your checking account is to mark all the cleared transactions.

Cleared Transactions Transactions recorded in the Check Register that have already been processed by the bank. These may include deposits, checks (withdrawals), ATM transactions, and so on.

To mark cleared transactions, follow these steps:

1. After you enter information from your bank statement, QuickBooks displays a list of uncleared transactions. Use the arrow keys to move the arrow to each transaction that appears on your bank statement.

2. For each transaction, press Enter to mark the transaction as cleared. QuickBooks enters an asterisk (*) in the C field (next to the Num field) to show that the transaction has cleared. To unmark a transacton, move the arrow to the transaction and press the Spacebar.

Marking a Range of Cleared Transactions   If an uninterrupted sequence of checks appears on your bank statement, you can mark the range as cleared without marking each individual check. Just press F8 to display the Mark Range of Check Numbers as Cleared window, type the beginning and ending check numbers you want to mark as cleared, and press Enter. QuickBooks enters an asterisk (*) beside each check in the range.

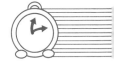

Entering Missing Transactions   If you find a transaction on your bank statement that you have not entered in the Check Register, you can enter it without leaving the reconciliation. Press F9 to go to the Check Register, enter the transaction as usual, and press F9 again to return to the uncleared transaction list.

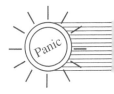

Completing the Reconciliation

You can complete the reconciliation after you have marked all cleared transactions. To complete the reconciliation:

1. Review the RECONCILIATION SUMMARY at the bottom of the uncleared transaction list. If the difference is zero, then your account balances, and you may complete the reconciliation. If the difference is a value other than zero (see the next section), then you need to either find the difference or have QuickBooks adjust your Check Register balance to agree with the statement balance.

2. If your checking account balances, press Ctrl-F10.

3. QuickBooks displays a congratulatory message and asks if you want to print a reconciliation report.

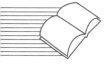

   Reconciliation Report   A list of the bank's beginning and ending balances, which reconciles them with cleared checks, payments, deposits, and other credits. Also listed are all uncleared transactions. You can only print the reconciliation immediately after you complete the current reconciliation, or just before you begin the next one.

4. If you want to print the reconciliation report, type Y and press Enter. (Note: You do not have to print the report to complete the bank reconciliation.)

5. QuickBooks displays the Print Reconciliation Report window. If your printer is not shown, press Ctrl-L to select your printer from the list, and press Enter.

6. If you want the report's reconcile date to be other than the current date, type your chosen date. Press Enter.

7. Type a report title, if desired, and press Enter.

8. If you want a detailed report, change the s to f.

9. Press Ctrl-Enter to print the reconciliation report.

Adjusting for Differences

If the difference shown in the Reconciliation Summary is a value other than zero, you can go back through the transactions to try to locate the difference or have QuickBooks adjust your Check Register for the difference. To have Quickbooks make this adjustment:

1. From the uncleared transaction list, press Ctrl-F10.

2. QuickBooks displays the Create Opening Balance Adjustment window (for a difference in the opening balance) or the Problem window (which informs you of a reconciliation difference and its amount).

3. To adjust for an opening balance difference, type y, followed by the account you want to assign to the adjustment (in the Create Opening Balance Adjustment window). Then press Enter.

   To adjust for other differences, press Enter at the Problem window. QuickBooks displays the Adding Balance Adjustment Entry window. Type y, followed by the account you want to assign to the adjustment. Press Ctrl-Enter or F10 to enter the adjustment.

Lesson 14
Writing Invoices

In this lesson, you will learn how to use QuickBooks to write customer invoices.

Invoicing Your Customers

With QuickBooks, it's easy to write customer invoices and print them in just seconds (see Lesson 15). QuickBooks' invoices look professional and ensure consistency from invoice to invoice and customer to customer. When you write an invoice, QuickBooks updates your Accounts Receivable register automatically, so it reflects your outstanding invoices and balances due from customers.

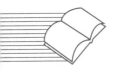

Accounts Receivable Register   When you select the Accounts Receivable account (an asset account that keeps track of your customers' outstanding balances) from the Chart Of Accounts window, the Accounts Receivable register is displayed.

Accessing the Write Invoices Screen

Use the Write Invoices screen to write actual customer invoices (which it resembles). To access the Write Invoices screen, follow these steps:

1. Select the Invoicing/Receivables option from the QuickBooks Main menu.

2. QuickBooks displays the Invoicing/Receivables menu. Select the Write/Print Invoices option to display the Write Invoices screen (shown in Figure 14.1).

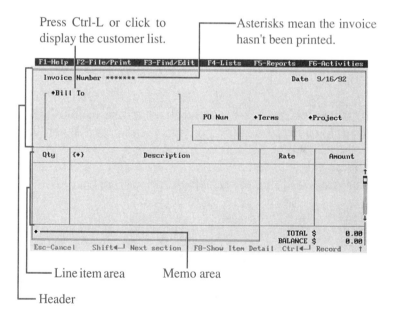

Figure 14.1   The Write Invoices screen. This is a Professional Invoice in Detail view.

Selecting the Type of Invoice to Use

The first time you access the Write Invoices screen, QuickBooks asks which type of invoice you want to use and provides three types:

- Service for service-oriented businesses that do not sell products (such as interior design, house painting, and gardening).

- Professional for businesses that provide professional services (such as accounting, legal, and medical).

- Product for businesses that sell products (such as auto parts, computers, and books).

To select the type of invoice you want to use, follow these steps:

1. Enter the invoice type you want to use in the Select Invoice Type window, or press Ctrl-L and select the type of invoice from the list.

2. Press Ctrl-Enter to select the invoice type. QuickBooks displays a blank copy of the selected invoice type in the Write Invoices screen.

Changing Invoice Types Don't worry if you find you need to use a different invoice type later. You can change the one you are using by changing the Invoice type company option. (Lesson 24 explains setting company options.)

Changing the Invoice View

QuickBooks displays invoices in one of two views: Detail or Printing. The *Detail view* of an invoice shows fields that prove useful when writing the invoice, but useless to your customer. The *Printing view* of an invoice shows how the invoice looks when printed. (Figure 14.1 shows a Professional invoice in Detail view.)

To change the Write Invoices screen from Detail to Printing view, press F8.

Writing an Invoice

Before you begin writing invoices, enter your customers, employees, line items, parts and services, customer types, payment terms, shipping methods, and invoice memos in the appropriate company lists. Using lists makes writing invoices more efficient and ensures that they are consistent. (See Lesson 6 to learn how to enter items in company lists.)

To write an invoice, follow these steps:

1. Access the Write Invoices screen. QuickBooks enters asterisks (*) in the Invoice Number field to indicate when an invoice hasn't been printed. Press F8 (if necessary) to change the invoice to the Detail view.

2. If you want to show a different date on the invoice, move to the Date field, and enter a new date. You can also use the + or – keys to change the date, one day at a time.

3. Press Tab to move to the Bill To field. Type the customer name, or press Ctrl-L to display the Customer List and choose a customer from the list.

Customer Not Found If you enter a customer name that does not appear in the Customer List, QuickBooks displays the Customer Not Found window and allows you to add the customer (or select another customer from the list). Press 1 to add the customer or 2 to select another customer.

4. If necessary, type the customer's address in the Bill To field. For Product invoices, QuickBooks completes the Ship To field automatically, provided you entered this information when you added the customer to the Customer List. (The Ship To field is not shown on Professional or Service invoices.)

5. Press Tab to move to the PO Num field; enter the customer's purchase order number (if applicable), and press Enter.

6. In the next field, press Ctrl-L to access the Payment Terms list; select the payment terms you are providing this customer, and press Enter.

7. For product invoices, the product invoice's header includes fields for the sales rep (Rep), shipping date (Ship), shipping method (Via), and shipping site (FOB). For each field preceded by a black diamond, press Ctrl-L to select an item from a company list. In the Ship field, enter the date that the product was shipped to the customer.

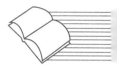

Parts of the Invoice   QuickBooks invoices consist of two parts: the *header* and the *line item area.* In the header, you enter customer information, payment terms, projects, and so on. You enter the items for which you are billing your customer in the line item area. Add messages to your customer in the memo area.

8. If you want to assign a project to the invoice transaction, press Ctrl-L in the Project field to select a project from the list, and then press Enter.

In the next part of the invoice, the line item area, you enter the items for which you are billing your customer. The next section explains how to complete the line item area of the invoice.

Entering Line Items in Invoices

After you enter the customer information in the header of the invoice, fill in the line item area of the invoice by following these steps:

1. Place the cursor in the line item area of the invoice. You can add up to 30 line items on the invoice.

2. At the Qty field, type the quantity of parts, merchandise, or hours for which you are billing your customer. Press Enter.

3. Press Ctrl-L to display the Item List shown in Figure 14.2. Use the Up and Down arrow keys to move the arrow to the line item you want, and press Enter. Note that you cannot enter the following line items on an invoice, unless you select them from the Item List: Subtotal, Refund, Payment, and Sales Tax.

101

Fill in the line item area of the invoice by selecting from the item list.

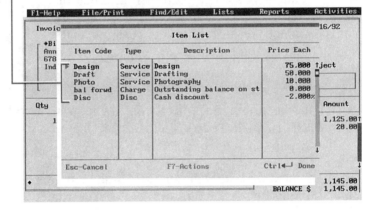

F1-Help	File/Print	Find/Edit	Lists	Reports	Activities

Invoic   16/92

Item List

Item Code	Type	Description	Price Each
Design	Service	Design	75.000 ↑ject
Draft	Service	Drafting	50.000
Photo	Service	Photography	10.000
bal forwd	Charge	Outstanding balance on st	0.000
Disc	Disc	Cash discount	-2.000%

Qty   Amount

1   1,125.00↑
                                                                      20.00

Esc-Cancel   F7-Actions   Ctrl◄─┘ Done

                                                         1,145.00
                                          BALANCE $ 1,145.00

Figure 14.2   Use the Item List to fill in the line item area of the invoice.

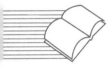

Line Items   Line items describe the product, merchandise, or service you sell to your customer. Line items also identify discounts, markups, sales tax, refunds, payments, and subtotals. When you add an item to the Item List, you assign an *item code* (which distinguishes one line item from another and links line items to income, expense, or balance sheet accounts). When you enter a line item on an invoice, QuickBooks assigns the amount to the appropriate income, expense, or balance sheet account automatically.

4. Move to the next line in the line item area of the invoice. Note that QuickBooks multiplies the quantity by the

Rate or Price Each as soon as you provide this information, and enters the result in the Amount field. The program updates the TOTAL and BALANCE fields each time a new line item appears in the Amount field.

5. Continue entering line items into the invoice's line item area.

6. When the line item area of the invoice is complete, press Shift-Enter to move to the Memo field, and press Ctrl-L to select a memo from the Invoice Memo List. After QuickBooks inserts the memo you selected, you can edit it as you like.

Inserting and Deleting Line Items   Provided you have less than 30 line items, you can insert another line item within the line item area. Position the cursor on the line directly after which you want to insert a line, and press Ctrl-I (to select the Insert Line Item option). QuickBooks inserts a blank line. You can also delete lines within the line item area. Position the cursor on the line you want to delete, and press Ctrl-D. QuickBooks deletes the line item and recalculates the invoice.

Recording an Invoice

After the header and line item area of the invoice are complete, and you've entered an invoice memo, you must record the invoice so its information is saved. To record the invoice, press Ctrl-Enter or F10. QuickBooks removes the invoices from the screen and displays a blank invoice.

Memorizing Invoices As with other transactions, QuickBooks can memorize invoices so you can recall them later and avoid typing the same information over and over again. To memorize an invoice, press Ctrl-M (to select the Memorize Invoice option), and enter a title or phrase that describes the invoice. To recall a memorized invoice, display a blank invoice, press Ctrl-T (to select the Recall Invoice option), and select the memorized invoice you want to recall from the Memorized Invoice Transaction List.

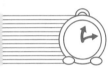

Using Invoice Groups If you normally write recurring invoices at the same time, you can group them by creating *invoice groups* (in much the same way you create transaction groups). Then you can enter the invoice groups at regular intervals and save time. Lesson 12 shows you how to use transaction groups; follow the same steps to set up and use invoice groups.

Editing an Invoice

Before you print invoices, you should review them to ensure that the customer information is correct, the invoice shows the proper payment terms, the line items are accurate and complete, and the invoice memo is appropriate. To edit an invoice, follow these steps:

1. Display the invoice you want to edit, using the following keys:

   Ctrl-PgUp to display the preceding invoice.

Ctrl-PgDn to display the next invoice.

Ctrl-Home to display the first invoice.

Ctrl-End to display the last invoice (a blank invoice).

2. Make the necessary changes to the field(s) in the invoice.

3. Press Ctrl-Enter or F10 to record the changes.

Deleting an Invoice

You can delete an invoice you wrote inadvertently or for practice. For the sake of your records, however, you should not delete an invoice with errors, one to which you have already applied a payment, one for a product that the customer subsequently cancels or returns, or one the customer paid with a check that was returned for insufficient funds.

To delete an invoice, follow these steps:

1. Display the invoice you want to delete, using the keys listed in the "Editing an Invoice" section of this lesson.

2. Press Ctrl-Del to select the Delete Invoice option from the Find/Edit menu.

3. Press Enter or 1 to delete the invoice. QuickBooks removes the invoice from the Write Invoices screen, and the invoice transaction from the Accounts Receivable register.

In the next lesson, you will learn how to print invoices and statements.

Printing Invoices and Statements

In this lesson, you will learn how to print invoices written at the Write Invoices screen, and customer statements.

Ordering Invoices and Other Supplies

If you plan to print invoices using QuickBooks, you should order preprinted invoices from Intuit, publisher of QuickBooks. Intuit offers invoices to fit continuous-feed and single-sheet (such as laser and inkjet) printers. Sample invoices are included in your QuickBooks package. Intuit also offers preprinted statements (though you can print statements on blank paper or your company's letterhead), and mailing labels.

To order invoices, statements, or mailing labels, complete the order form included in your QuickBooks package, or refer to Lesson 8 to learn how to print an order form from the QuickBooks program.

Preparing to Print Invoices

Preprinted invoices must be properly aligned in your printer before you start printing. Once the invoices are aligned, you can print statements with no additional adjustments. QuickBooks can print on continuous-feed or laser invoices. To prepare to print invoices, follow these steps:

1. Insert blank invoices into your printer.

2. Turn on your printer and make sure it is on-line.

3. Access the Write Invoices screen (see Lesson 14). Make sure you have at least one invoice to print.

4. Select the Print Invoices option from the File/Print menu or press Ctrl-P.

5. QuickBooks displays the Print Invoices window (shown in Figure 15.1).

Make sure the correct paper type and printer are selected.

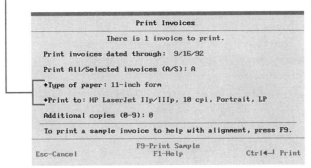

```
                        Print Invoices

                  There is 1 invoice to print.

      Print invoices dated through:  9/16/92

      Print All/Selected invoices (A/S): A

    ◆Type of paper: 11-inch form

    ◆Print to: HP LaserJet IIp/IIIp, 10 cpi, Portrait, LP

      Additional copies (0-9): 0

      To print a sample invoice to help with alignment, press F9.

                        F9-Print Sample
      Esc-Cancel          F1-Help              Ctrl◄┘ Print
```

Figure 15.1   The Print Invoices window. From here you can align or print invoices.

Aligning Continuous-Feed Invoices

To position continuous-feed invoices in your printer:

1. Follow the steps for preparing to print invoices.

2. At the Print Invoices window, press Tab twice to move to the Type of paper field. Press Ctrl-L to display the available paper types; select the type of paper you are testing, and press Enter.

3. If your printer does not appear in the Print to field, press Ctrl-L to display the printer list, choose a printer from the list, and press Enter.

4. Press F9. Do not adjust your printer at this time.

5. Press Enter to print the sample invoice. QuickBooks displays the Automatic Form Alignment window.

6. Review the sample invoice; if it prints correctly, go to step 12. If it does not print correctly, check the POINTER LINE arrow's position number, and type it in the Position number field. Press Enter. If the horizontal positioning is not correct because the type is too spread out or compressed, you may need to adjust your printer settings.

7. QuickBooks prints a second sample invoice. Review the invoice. If the vertical positioning is still not correct, use the knob on the side of your printer to adjust the invoices. Note the position of the invoices in your printer, so you can align them correctly next time.

8. When the invoices are correctly aligned (at the Automatic Form Alignment window), press Enter. QuickBooks returns to the Print Invoices window.

Positioning Laser Invoices

To print a sample laser invoice to ensure alignment:

1. Follow the steps for preparing to print invoices.

2. At the Print Invoices window, press Tab twice to move to the Type of paper field. Press Ctrl-L to display the available paper types; select the type of paper you are testing, and press Enter.

3. If your laser printer does not appear in the Print to field, press Ctrl-L to display the printer list, choose a printer from the list, and press Enter.

4. Press F9.

5. Press Enter to print the sample invoice. QuickBooks displays the Automatic Form Alignment window.

6. Review the sample invoice. If the type on the sample invoice is too far to the left, increase the number in the Starting position field of the Automatic Alignment window. If the type is too far to the right, decrease the number in the Starting position field.

7. Press Enter to print another sample invoice.

Printing Invoices

When your invoices are properly positioned, you're ready to print your QuickBooks invoices. To print invoices:

1. Follow the steps for preparing to print invoices.

2. At the `Print invoices dated through` field in the Print Invoices window, type the date through which you want invoices printed, and press Enter.

3. At the `Print All/Selected invoices` field, type **s** if you want to select which invoices to print; otherwise, leave the setting at **A** to print all invoices. Press Enter.

4. Press Ctrl-L at the `Type of paper` field to display the available paper types; select the type of paper you are using to print invoices, and press Enter.

5. If your printer does not appear in the `Print to` field, press Ctrl-L to display the printer list, choose a printer from the list, and press Enter.

6. In the `Additional copies` field, type the number of extra copies of each invoice you want to print.

7. Press Ctrl-Enter or F10.

8. If you typed **s** in the `Print All/Selected invoices` field, QuickBooks displays the Select Invoices to Print window. See the next section to learn how to select invoices to print.

9. QuickBooks next displays the Set Invoice Number window shown in Figure 15.2.

Change the invoice number here.

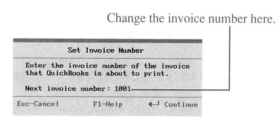

Figure 15.2 The Set Invoice Number window.

10. If the invoice number is incorrect, type the number of the next blank invoice. You can use the + or – keys to change the invoice number, one at a time.

11. Press F9 to print the first invoice only, or press Ctrl-Enter to begin printing all invoices.

Duplicate Invoice Numbers   If you have a duplicate invoice number, QuickBooks displays a warning and shows you the original invoice information assigned to that invoice number. Press Y to print the invoice with the duplicate number or N to go back to the Set Invoice Number (where you can change the invoice number).

12. After invoices are printed, QuickBooks asks whether they printed correctly. If they did, press Enter. If they did not, select No, and type the first invoice number that did not print correctly. QuickBooks marks the first invoice that did not print correctly—and the following invoices—with asterisks (*) in the Invoice number field so they can be reprinted.

Reprinting Invoices   If you find an error on a printed invoice, reprint the invoice by displaying the invoice and typing an asterisk (*) over the existing invoice number. Then press Ctrl-Enter or F10 to record the change and print the invoice as usual.

Selecting Invoices to Print

Unless you specify otherwise, QuickBooks prints (in the Print Invoices window) all invoices dated on or before the date you enter. To select invoices to print, follow these steps:

1. At the Print Invoices window, type s in the Print All/ Selected invoices field.

2. After you complete the other fields in the Print Invoice window, press Ctrl-Enter or F10.

3. QuickBooks displays the Select Invoices to Print window. Use the arrow keys to move the arrow to an invoice you don't want to print (initially, all invoices are marked to print), and press the Spacebar. Press the Spacebar again to deselect an invoice; press Ctrl-Spacebar to select or deselect all invoices.

4. Press Ctrl-Enter or F10 to begin printing invoices.

Printing Statements

A *statement* contains a summary of the invoices you have sent to a customer, payments received, and the balance forward for a specified period of time. At the bottom of the statement, QuickBooks prints a Customer Aging Status Schedule that divides the amount due into time periods. Statements cannot be viewed on-screen. You can print statements on Intuit's preprinted forms, your company letterhead, or blank paper, provided the paper is 8 1/2 inches wide by 11 inches long. Letterhead type must not exceed the top 1.9 inches of paper, and cannot include type at the bottom of the page. To print a statement:

1. Insert preprinted invoices, letterhead, or blank paper in your printer as usual.

2. Turn on your printer and make sure it is on-line.

3. Access the Write Invoices screen, as explained in an earlier lesson.

4. Select the Print Statements option from the File/Print menu.

5. QuickBooks displays the Print Statements window.

6. Enter the period through which you want statements printed, whether you want to select the customers to include, and whether to restrict statements (to customers with past-due balances, or balances greater than a specified amount).

7. If your printer does not appear in the `Print to` field, press Ctrl-L to display the printer list; choose a printer from the list. Press Enter.

8. Press Ctrl-L at the `Type of paper` field to display the available paper types. Select a paper type and press Enter.

9. In the `Additional copies` field, type the number of extra copies of each statement you want to print.

10. Press Ctrl-Enter or F10 to print statements.

Lesson 16

Receiving and Depositing Customer Payments

In this lesson, you will learn how to enter payments from customers, and make a deposit in QuickBooks to record the payments.

Entering Customer Payments

You enter payments from your customers in the Receive Payments screen. QuickBooks then applies payments to invoices, prepares deposits, and updates the Accounts Receivable account. To enter a customer payment:

1. Select the Invoicing/Receivables option from the QuickBooks Main menu.

2. From the Invoicing/Receivables menu, select the Receive Payments option.

3. QuickBooks displays the RECEIVE PAYMENTS screen shown in Figure 16.1.

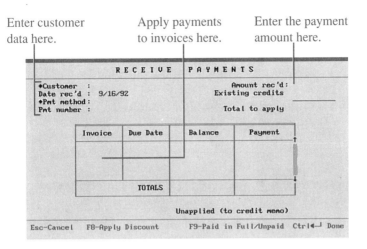

Enter customer data here.   Apply payments to invoices here.   Enter the payment amount here.

Figure 16.1   Use the RECEIVE PAYMENTS screen to enter customer payments.

4. Type the customer's name in the Customer field, or press Ctrl-L to select the customer from the Customer List. QuickBooks completes the Existing credits field, and enters all outstanding invoices (including the invoice number, due date, and balance for each).

5. Move to the Amount field, and type the amount you received from the customer. Press Enter. QuickBooks subtracts the existing credits from the amount received, and enters the result in the Total to apply field.

6. If the date in the Date rec'd field is incorrect, type a new date (or press the + or – keys to change the date one day at a time). Press Enter.

7. At the Pmt method field, press Ctrl-L to display a list of payment methods. Select a method and press Enter.

8. Type a payment number or the customer's check number in the Pmt number field. Press Enter. Next, you must apply the customer's payment to outstanding invoices (see the next section).

Applying Payments to Invoices

To apply customer payments to outstanding invoices:

1. Complete the top portion of the RECEIVE PAYMENTS screen, as explained in the previous section of this lesson.

2. Position the cursor in the Payment field of the appropriate invoice(s), and change the invoice amount to which you do not want to apply payment. Press F9 to set the invoice back to unpaid (0.00). Press F9 again to set the invoice to paid in full. Note that QuickBooks applies the payment to the oldest invoice first, then the next oldest, and so on, automatically.

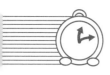

Changing Payment Application Methods By default, QuickBooks applies payments to invoices using the *balance forward* method (oldest invoice first, then next oldest, and so on). You can change the payment method to the *open item* method, which enables you to apply payments to specific invoices. Change the payment application method by setting the company option that controls the application of payment (see Lesson 22).

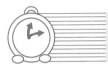

Overpayments   If you receive a payment for more than the customer owes, the Unapplied field in the RECEIVE PAYMENTS screen reflects the overpayment. When you record the payment, QuickBooks asks if you want to create a *credit memo* (an invoice that adjusts the customer's outstanding balance); press Enter to create one. Overpayments appear in the Accounts Receivable register, with the word OPEN in the Paid column. The next time you receive a payment from the customer, QuickBooks enters the overpayment or credit memo amount in the Existing credits field in the RECEIVE PAYMENTS screen.

Applying Discounts

You can apply one discount to each customer invoice as you enter payments. To apply a discount, follow these steps:

1. Complete the top portion of the RECEIVE PAYMENTS screen, as explained earlier in this lesson.

2. Position the cursor on the invoice to which you want to apply a discount, and press F8.

3. QuickBooks displays the Apply Discount window shown in Figure 16.2.

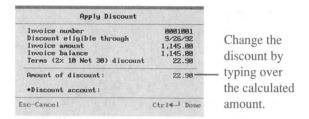

Figure 16.2 Use the Apply Discount window to apply a discount to a customer invoice.

4. QuickBooks calculates the discount, based on the discount terms granted to the customer. Change the discount, if necessary, by typing over the amount in the Amount of discount field. Press Enter.

5. At the Discount account field, press Ctrl-L to select the account to which you want to assign the discount.

6. Press Ctrl-Enter or F10 to return to the RECEIVE PAYMENTS screen. QuickBooks enters an asterisk (*) next to the invoice that has been discounted.

7. Press F9 to apply the payment to the discounted invoice amount.

Recording Payments

After you have entered a payment and applied discounts (if any) to customer invoices, record the payment in the RECEIVE PAYMENTS screen by pressing Ctrl-Enter or F10. QuickBooks records the payment, and displays a blank RECEIVE PAYMENTS screen so you can enter another customer's payment.

Making Deposits

After you enter and record customer payments, you must make a deposit in QuickBooks; then payments are recorded in the Accounts Receivable register, and the deposit of funds is recorded in your checking account. To make a deposit in QuickBooks:

1. Select Invoicing/Receivables from the Main menu.

2. From the Invoicing/Receivables menu, select Make Deposits. QuickBooks displays the DEPOSIT SUMMARY window. You can also access the DEPOSIT SUMMARY window from the Write Invoices screen (or the Accounts Receivable register) by selecting Make Deposits from the Activities menu.

3. Enter the date you want QuickBooks to use to record the deposit in the Deposit field. Press Enter.

4. At the Account for deposit field, press Ctrl-L to select your checking or other bank account into which you want the deposit recorded. Press Enter.

5. In the Payments List, use the Arrow keys to move the arrow to the payment(s) you want to include in the deposit. Press the Spacebar to include the payment; press the Spacebar again to exclude the payment. You can include up to 46 payments in each deposit transaction.

6. Press Ctrl-Enter or F10 to make the deposit.

Printing a Deposit Summary

To print a deposit summary you can use as a deposit slip:

1. At the DEPOSIT SUMMARY window, move the arrow to each payment type, and press Ctrl-Spacebar to include all payments of that type. Repeat this step until you have marked all payments to include in the deposit.

2. Press Ctrl-P.

3. QuickBooks displays the Select Printer to Use window. If your printer does not appear, press Ctrl-L to select your printer.

4. Press Enter to print the Deposit Summary.

Lesson 17

Using the Accounts Receivable Register

In this lesson, you will learn how to use the Accounts Receivable register to enter new transactions and edit or delete existing transactions.

Accessing the Accounts Receivable Register

The Accounts Receivable register looks similar to the Check Register. QuickBooks keeps track of the money your customers owe by entering transactions in the Accounts Receivable register each time you write an invoice, issue a credit memo, apply a discount to an invoice, or make a deposit for payment from a customer. To access the Accounts Receivable register:

1. Select Invoicing/Receivables from the QuickBooks Main menu.

2. From the Invoicing/Receivables menu, select the View A/R Register option.

3. QuickBooks displays the Accounts Receivable register shown in Figure 17.1.

Select the invoice option to enter an invoice in
the Write Invoices screen.

F1-Help	F2-File/Print		F3-Find/Edit	F4-Lists	F5-Reports	F6-Activities
DATE	NUMBER		CUSTOMER	DUE	BILLINGS	RECEIPTS
			BEGINNING			
9/16/92	1001	Ann Adams		PAID	1,145 00	
9/16/92	5689	Ann Adams				1,500 00
9/16/92		Ann Adams		OPEN	0 00	
			<NEW TRANSACTION>			
		1. Invoice ▶ 2. Receipt				

Receivables
Esc-Leave   ◄┘ Edit   Ending Balance: $-355.00

Select the Receipt option to record a customer payment in the
Receive Payments screen.

Figure 17.1   The Accounts Receivable register.

Quick Access   You can also access the Accounts
Receivable register directly from the Write Invoices screen by pressing Ctrl-R.

Entering New Transactions

You cannot enter a transaction directly in the Accounts
Receivable register. You can, however, enter an invoice
or a customer payment in the Write Invoices screen, or
record a customer payment in the Receive Payments screen,
and you can access these from the Accounts Receivable
register.

To enter a new transaction in the Accounts Receivable register, follow these steps:

1. Access the Accounts Receivable register as explained above.

2. Press Ctrl-End to highlight the <NEW TRANSACTION> line.

3. Press 1 to display the Write Invoices screen (to enter an invoice), or press 2 to display the Receive Payments screen (to enter a customer payment).

4. Enter and record the new transaction, and then press Esc to return to the Accounts Receivable register.

Editing and Deleting Transactions

To edit a transaction from the Accounts Receivable register, follow these steps:

1. Access the Accounts Receivable register as explained earlier in this lesson.

2. Highlight the transaction you want to edit. (Lesson 9 lists the shortcuts for moving through a register.)

3. Select Edit Transaction from the Find/Edit menu or press Ctrl-E.

4. QuickBooks displays the Write Invoices screen if you selected an invoice or credit memo transaction, the Receive Payments screen if you selected a payment transaction, or the Deposit Summary window if you selected a deposit transaction.

5. Make any necessary changes and press Ctrl-Enter or
   F10. Then press Esc to return to the Accounts Receivable register.

To delete a transaction from the Accounts Receivable
register, follow these steps:

1. Access the Accounts Receivable register as explained
   earlier in this lesson.

2. Highlight the transaction you want to delete.

3. Select Delete Transaction from the Find/Edit menu, or
   press Ctrl-Del.

4. QuickBooks displays the Write Invoices screen if you
   selected an invoice or credit memo transaction, the
   Receive Payments screen if you selected a payment
   transaction, or the Deposit Summary window if you
   selected a deposit transaction. The OK to Delete Transaction window is also displayed.

5. Press 1 to delete the transaction. QuickBooks returns to
   the Accounts Receivable register.

Viewing a Transaction History

At the Accounts Receivable register, you can view a *transaction history*, which shows all transactions (in chronological order) in the register related to the selected transaction.

To view a transaction history, follow these steps:

1. Access the Accounts Receivable register as explained
   earlier in this lesson.

2. Highlight the transaction for which you want to view the transaction history.

3. Select the Transaction History option from the Find/ Edit menu, or press Ctrl-H.

4. QuickBooks displays the Transaction History window for the transaction.

To view a transaction within the Transaction History window, follow these steps:

1. Move the arrow to the transaction and press Enter.

2. QuickBooks highlights the selected transaction in the Accounts Receivable register. Press Ctrl-H to view your selection's transaction history.

3. Press Esc to remove the Transaction History window from the screen.

Adding Customer Notes at the Accounts Receivable Register You can add notes about a customer at the Accounts Receivable register by highlighting a transaction that contains the customer, pressing Ctrl-N (to select the Notepad option), and typing your note. Press Ctrl-Enter or F10 to save the customer note.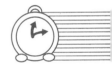

In the next lesson, you will learn how to pay your bills with QuickBooks.

Paying Bills

In this lesson you will learn how to pay bills in the
Accounts Payable register.

Working with the Accounts Payable Register

The liabilities you owe to vendors for goods and services to
run your business are called *accounts payable*. The
QuickBooks Accounts Payable register helps you track
your accounts payable and pay them on a timely basis.
QuickBooks reminds you when bills are due and enables
you to select bills to pay directly from the Accounts Payable
register. When you tell QuickBooks to pay bills, payment
transactions are recorded in the Accounts Payable register;
check transactions are recorded in the Check Register,
ready to print.

Accessing the Accounts Payable Register

To access the Accounts Payable register:

1. Select the Accounts Payable option from the
   QuickBooks Main menu.

2. From the Accounts Payable menu, select A/P Register. Note that QuickBooks is about to access the payable account shown next to the A/P Register line (Payables) in the Accounts Payable menu. An Accounts Payable register is also available for the sales tax account (Sales Tax).

3. QuickBooks displays the Accounts Payable register shown in Figure 18.1.

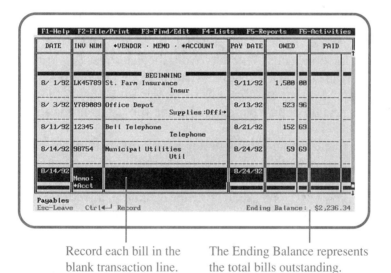

Record each bill in the blank transaction line.

The Ending Balance represents the total bills outstanding.

Figure 18.1   Use the Accounts Payable register to enter and pay bills.

Entering Bills

Entering bills in the Accounts Payable register is similar to entering transactions in the Check Register (see Lesson 9). To enter a bill in the Accounts Payable register, follow these steps:

1. Access the Accounts Payable register as explained above.

2. Press Ctrl-End to highlight the last empty transaction line.

3. If the date the bill is received is different, type over the existing date in the Date field. Press Enter.

4. At the Inv Num field, type the number of the vendor's invoice, and press Enter.

5. At the Vendor field, press Ctrl-L to display the Vendor List and select a vendor from the list. Press Enter. You can also type a vendor's name. If QuickBooks does not find your vendor's name in the Vendor List, you can add it at this time (or select another vendor from the list).

6. QuickBooks fills in the Pay Date field on the basis of the date you receive the bill. The pay date is calculated using the default number of days (10). If necessary, change the pay date by entering a new date, or use the + or – keys to change the date one day at a time. Press Enter.

Changing the Calculated Pay Date QuickBooks calculates the date bills should be paid, based on the date the transaction occurs and the program's default number of days (10). You can change the default number of days by changing one of the company options (Default Number of Days Between DATE and PAY DATE in Accounts Payable). Lesson 23 explains changing company options.

7. Type the amount of the bill in the Owed field, and press Enter.

8. Type a memo, if desired, and press Enter.

9. At the Account field, type the name of the account you want to assign to the bill, or press Ctrl-L to select an account from the Chart Of Accounts list. If you want to record a transfer from one QuickBooks balance sheet account to another, you can enter the destination balance sheet account in the Account field. If you want to assign more than one account to the bill, split the transaction by pressing Ctrl-S to open the Split Transaction window. (Lesson 10 explained splitting transactions.)

10. If you want to assign a project to the bill, press Tab to move to the Project field (displayed only if the project tracking option is turned on). Press Ctrl-L to select a project from the Project List.

11. Record the bill in the Accounts Payable register by pressing Ctrl-Enter or F10.

Memorizing Bills   As a shortcut for entering recurring bills (such as office rent, insurance premiums, service contracts, and so forth), you can memorize bill transactions with QuickBooks, and recall them later in the Accounts Payable register. Bills are memorized the same way as transactions in the Check Register (see Lesson 11).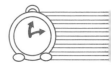

Using Transaction Groups for Bills   If you have a group of bills for which you don't receive invoices or statements, and they are due the same time each month, you can use transaction groups to enter them all at once into the Accounts Payable register. See Lesson 12 to learn how to set up and execute a transaction group.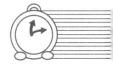

Changing or Deleting Paid Bills   If you're changing the amount of a paid bill (or deleting a paid bill), QuickBooks will not allow you to record the change or delete the bill until you delete the payment applied to the bill. To find the payment transaction, press Ctrl-H to display the transaction history for the bill, highlight the payment transaction, and press Enter. Then delete the payment (as explained later in this lesson).

Paying Bills

When you pay bills from the Accounts Payable register, QuickBooks enters a payment transaction in that register— as well as a check transaction in the Check Register, with asterisks (*) in the check number field to indicate the check is ready to be printed. To pay bills from the Accounts Payable register:

1. Select the Accounts Payable option from the QuickBooks Main menu.

2. Select the Pay Bills option from the Accounts Payable menu.

3. QuickBooks displays the Pay Vendors window (shown in Figure 18.2).

Accessing the Pay Vendors Window from the Accounts Payable Register   If you're at the Accounts Payable register and want to pay bills, select the Pay Bills option from the Activities menu, or press Ctrl-Y.

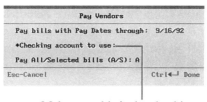

Make sure this is the checking
account you use to write checks.

Figure 18.2   The Pay Vendors window.

4. Type the date through which you want to pay bills, or change the date using the + or – keys. Press Enter.

5. At the `Checking account to use` field, press Ctrl-L to select the checking account from which you want to pay bills. Press Enter.

6. In the last field, type `s` to select which bills you want to pay, or whether you want to make partial payments.

7. Press Ctrl-Enter or F10. QuickBooks displays the Choose Bills to Pay window.

8. To pay a bill in full, position the cursor on the `Payment` field for the bill, and press F9. Press F9 again if you don't want to pay a bill listed in the Choose Bills to Pay window. To make a partial payment, type the amount of the payment in the `Payment` field.

9. Continue entering payments in the Choose Bills to Pay window.

10. Press Ctrl-Enter.

11. QuickBooks displays the Before Recording Payments window; this allows you to print a payment summary. Press 1 if you don't want to print a payment summary (this will take you to step 13); press 2 to print a payment summary.

12. QuickBooks displays the Select Printer or File window. If the printer you are using does not appear in the Print to field, press Ctrl-L to select another printer. Press Ctrl-Enter.

13. QuickBooks displays the Preparing to Record Checks window with today's date. Change the date, if necessary; press Ctrl-Enter or F10 to record payment transactions in the Accounts Payable register and check transactions in the Check Register.

14. If you print checks with QuickBooks, go to the Write Checks screen and press Ctrl-P. Follow the instructions for printing checks in Lesson 8.

Editing Payments

To edit a payment in the Accounts Payable register, follow these steps:

1. Access the Accounts Payable register.

2. Highlight the payment transaction you want to edit.

3. Select the Edit Payment option from the Find/Edit menu, or press Ctrl-E.

4. QuickBooks displays the Edit Payment window. Press Ctrl-L to change the checking account, if necessary, and press Enter.

5. QuickBooks next displays the Choose Bills to Pay window. Change the payment amount and press Ctrl-Enter.

6. Press 1 if you don't want to print a payment summary; to print a payment summary, press 2 and then press Enter.

7. Change the check date, if necessary, and press Enter. QuickBooks records the edited payment in the Accounts Payable register.

Deleting a Payment

To delete a payment (or unpaid bill transaction) in the Accounts Payable register, follow these steps:

1. Access the Accounts Payable register.

2. Highlight the payment you want to delete.

3. Select the Delete Transaction option from the Find/Edit menu, or press Ctrl-Del.

4. Press 1 to delete the payment.

In the next lesson you will learn how to use the Credit Card account in QuickBooks to track your credit card activity.

Lesson 19

Working with Credit Card Accounts

In this lesson you will learn how to use QuickBooks' Credit Card accounts to track your credit card activity.

Tracking Credit Card Transactions

If you use credit cards in your business, you can add a Credit Card account for each card you use; this will help you record and keep track of purchases, payments, and finance charges. You can reconcile your credit card statements and pay your bills using only a few keystrokes.

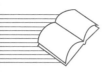

Credit Card Account A QuickBooks account used to enter credit card purchases and payments. A separate account should be set up for each of your credit cards (MasterCard, Visa, American Express, and so on).

Adding a Credit Card Account

Before you add a credit card account, add the credit card vendor to the Vendor List (see Lesson 6). To add a credit card account, follow these steps:

1. Access the Chart Of Accounts window, as explained in Lesson 5.

2. Press Ctrl-Ins to select the Add/New option and display the Select Type of Account to Add window.

3. Select the type of credit card account and press Enter.

4. QuickBooks displays the Add New Credit Card Account window as shown in Figure 19.1.

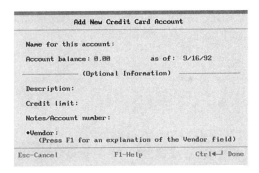

Figure 19.1 The Add New Credit Card Account window.

5. Complete the Name for this account field and press Enter. Account names can contain up to 15 characters, including letters and spaces.

6. Enter the amount you currently owe (as of your QuickBooks start date) in the Account balance field. Press Enter.

7. Type the date that relates to the account balance in the As of field, and press Enter.

8. Enter a description of the account and press Enter.

9. In the Credit limit field, type your credit card limit and press Enter.

10. Complete the optional Note/Account number field if you want.

11. At the Vendor field, press Ctrl-L to display the Vendor List; select the credit card company from the list.

12. Press Ctrl-Enter or F10 to add the credit card account to the Chart Of Accounts list.

Entering Credit Card Transactions

You enter credit card transactions in your credit card account the same way you enter transactions in the Checking account and Accounts Payable accounts. Enter credit card transactions throughout the month as you make purchases, or at the end of the month when you receive your monthly statement. To enter a credit card transaction, follow these steps:

1. Access the Chart Of Accounts window, as explained in Lesson 5.

2. Select the credit card account in which you want to enter transactions. QuickBooks displays the Credit Card register.

3. Press Ctrl-End to highlight the last empty transaction line.

4. Enter the credit card transactions the same way you enter transactions in the Check Register (see Lesson 9).

5. Press Ctrl-Enter or F10 to record the transaction.

Memorizing Credit Card Transactions   You can memorize and recall transactions in the Credit Card register the same way you do in the Check Register (refer to Lesson 11).

Reconciling and Paying Your Credit Card Account

QuickBooks reconciles your credit card account, and creates a transaction for any expenses shown on your credit card statement but not in the Credit Card register (such as finance charges or credit card fees). QuickBooks then gives you the option of paying the credit card company through a handwritten check or a QuickBooks check.

To reconcile and pay your Credit Card account, follow these steps:

1. From the Credit Card register, select the Reconcile/Pay option from the Activities menu or press Ctrl-Y.

2. QuickBooks displays the Credit Card Statement Information window shown in Figure 19.2.

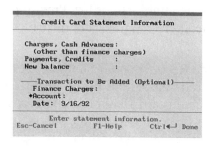

```
       Credit Card Statement Information

  Charges, Cash Advances:
    (other than finance charges)
  Payments, Credits     :
  New balance           :

   ——Transaction to Be Added (Optional)——
    Finance Charges:
    ◆Account:
    Date:  9/16/92

          Enter statement information.
  Esc-Cancel          F1-Help       Ctrl◄┘ Done
```

Figure 19.2   Use the Credit Card Statement Information window to enter information from your monthly statement.

3. Type the charges, cash advances, payments, credits, and new balance from your credit card statement, and press Enter.

4. Enter the finance charges shown on your statement, the account you want to assign to the finance charge transaction, and the date finance charges were assessed.

5. Press Ctrl-Enter to display the list of uncleared credit card transactions.

6. Use the arrow keys to move the arrow to each transaction that appears on your credit card statement. For each transaction, press the Enter key to mark the transaction as cleared. QuickBooks enters an asterisk (*) in the column next to the Reference column to show the transaction has cleared. Press F8 to mark a range of transactions as cleared (as you learned in Lesson 13).

Switching to the Credit Card Register   If you need to go back to the Credit Card register while you are reconciling your Credit Card account, press F9 from the uncleared transactions list. Press F9 again to return to the uncleared transactions list.

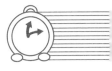

7. Review the Reconciliation Summary at the bottom of the uncleared transactions list. If the difference is zero, then your credit card account balances, and you may go on to step 8 and complete the reconciliation. If the difference is a value other than zero, then you need to either find the difference (press Esc) or have QuickBooks adjust your Credit Card register balance to agree with your credit card statement (press Enter at the Adjusting Register to Agree with Statement window).

8. If your credit card account balances, QuickBooks displays the Make Credit Card Payment window.

9. In the Bank account to use field, press Ctrl-L to select the checking account you will use to pay the credit card bill, and press Enter.

10. Type Y to write a manual check or type N if you're using QuickBooks to print checks.

11. Press Ctrl-Enter or F10 to process and record the payment in the Check Register and the Credit Card register; if you don't want to pay the credit card bill now, press Esc instead.

In the next lesson, you will learn how to use other balance sheet accounts in QuickBooks.

Lesson 20

Working with Other Balance Sheet Accounts

In this lesson, you will learn how to add balance sheet accounts in QuickBooks and update account balances.

Using Balance Sheet Accounts

In previous lessons in this book, you learned how to add a checking account, income and expense accounts, and a credit card account in QuickBooks. This lesson shows you how to add other balance sheet accounts, such as a current asset account, fixed asset account, current liability account, and so forth.

The following is a list of the types of balance sheet accounts you can add in your QuickBooks' Chart of Accounts, and what they track:

Account Type	Tracks
Checking	Transactions in checking, savings, and money market accounts.
Accounts receivable	Transactions between you and your customers, including invoices, payments from cus-

140

	tomers, refunds, credit memos, statements, and deposits.
Current asset	Notes receivable due within a year, and assets such as petty cash, prepaid expenses, inventory (though QuickBooks is not recommended for precise tracking of extensive inventory), security deposits, advances or notes receivable due in 12 months or less, and any other assets you need to convert to cash.
Fixed asset	Long-term notes and depreciable assets you use in your business.
Accounts payable	Outstanding bills.
Credit card	Lines of credit and credit card transactions.
Current liability	Liabilities that are scheduled to be paid within 12 months, such as payroll taxes, sales tax, accrued or deferred salaries, and notes payable.
Long-term liability	Liabilities scheduled to be paid over periods longer than 12 months, such as mortgages.
Equity	Owner's equity, including capital investment, capital stock, draws, and retained earnings.

Adding a Balance Sheet Account

To add a balance sheet account, follow these steps:

1. Select the Chart of Accounts option from the QuickBooks Main menu.

2. QuickBooks displays the Chart Of Accounts window. Press Ctrl-Ins to select the Add/New option and display the Select Type of Account To Add window.

3. Use the arrow keys to point to the type of account you want to add. Choose an account from the Assets Accounts list or the Liability Accounts list. Press Enter.

4. QuickBooks displays the Add New Account window. Figure 20.1 shows the Add New Current Asset Account window, used to add a current asset account.

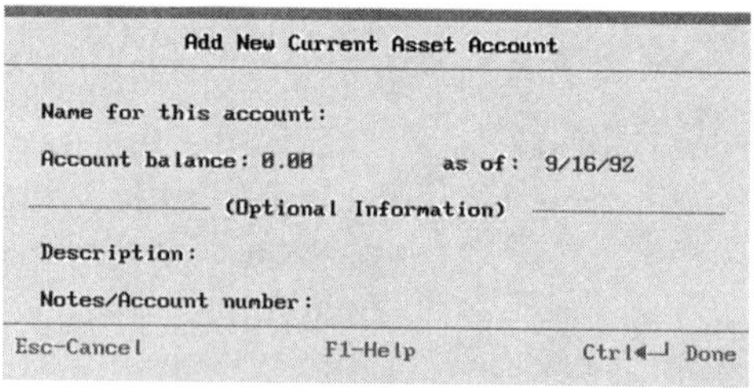

```
            Add New Current Asset Account

   Name for this account:

   Account balance: 0.00          as of: 9/16/92

   ─────────────── (Optional Information) ───────────
   Description:

   Notes/Account number:
   Esc-Cancel              F1-Help              Ctrl◄─┘ Done
```

Figure 20.1   Use the Add New Current Asset Account window to enter information about the Current Asset account you are adding.

5. Type the name of the account (using up to 15 characters, including numbers, letters, and spaces). Press Enter.

6. In the Account balance field, enter the opening balance for the account you are adding. Use the following guidelines to enter an opening balance:

Account Type	Opening Balance
Checking and savings	Dollar amount in the bank on the date you start QuickBooks or add the account.
Current asset	Value of the asset on your QuickBooks start date.
Fixed asset	Value of the asset on your QuickBooks start date.
Current liability	Loan balance on your QuickBooks start date.
Long-term liability	Loan balance on your QuickBooks start date.
Credit card	Dollar amount owed to the credit card company on your QuickBooks start date.
Owner's equity	Amount invested in the business as of your QuickBooks start date.
Accounts receivable	No opening balance entered; historical transactions entered to determine opening balance.
Accounts payable	No opening balance entered; historical transactions entered to determine opening balance.

If you're tracking multiple assets or liabilities in one account (for example, several pieces of equipment in a fixed asset account), enter zero as the opening balance.

Then enter individual transactions in the account register for each asset or liability.

7. Type the date that relates to the account balance you entered in step 6, and press Enter.

8. Enter an optional description of the account in the Description field. Press Enter.

9. Type a note or an account number in the Notes/Account number field.

10. Press Ctrl-Enter or F10 to add the balance sheet account to the QuickBooks Chart of Accounts.

Selecting an Account to Use

To record transactions or use the register for a balance sheet account, you must first select the account from the Chart of Accounts. When you select an account to use, QuickBooks displays the register for the account.

To select an account to use, follow these steps:

1. Select the Chart of Accounts option from the QuickBooks Main menu.

2. QuickBooks displays the Chart Of Accounts window. Note that QuickBooks places an asterisk (*) in the Type column for accounts that have items on which to act (such as checks to print, invoices to print, bills to pay, and so on).

3. Use the Up and Down arrow keys to point to the account with which you want to work, and press Enter.

QuickBooks displays the register for the account you select. Figure 20.2 shows the Current Asset account register.

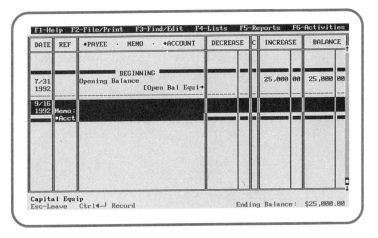

Figure 20.2 The Current Asset account register.

Entering Transactions in Accounts Enter transactions in balance sheet accounts, such as a Current Asset account or a Fixed Asset account, the same way you enter transactions in the Check Register (see Lesson 9). You can also memorize and split transactions in balance sheet accounts (see Lessons 10 and 11).

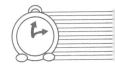

Updating Account Values

You occasionally may need to update the value of an asset or liability account so the ending balance in the account reflects the actual value of the asset or liability at a given date.

To update the value of an asset or liability account, follow these steps:

1. Select the account you want to update from the Chart Of Accounts window (as explained above).

2. Select the Update Acct Balance option from the Activities menu, or press Ctrl-Y.

3. QuickBooks displays the Update Account Balance window (see Figure 20.3).

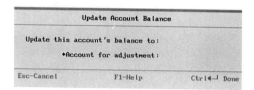

```
                    Update Account Balance

Update this account's balance to:
            •Account for adjustment:

Esc-Cancel                 F1-Help            Ctrl◄┘ Done
```

Figure 20.3 Use the Update Account Balance window to update the value of an account.

4. Type the amount to which you want to adjust the account balance, and press Enter.

5. In the next field, press Ctrl-L to select the income or expense account you want to assign to the adjustment transaction.

6. Press Ctrl-Enter or F10 to enter the adjustment in the account register and update the account balance.

In the next lesson, you will learn how to create and print QuickBooks reports.

Lesson 21
Creating and Printing Reports

In this lesson, you will learn how to create and print reports using QuickBooks.

Creating Reports

The QuickBooks program includes 13 preset reports that can be viewed on-screen or printed. In addition to the preset reports, QuickBooks includes two generic report types you can create or customize to fit your specific business needs. (See Lesson 22 for an explanation on customizing reports.) To create reports:

1. Select Reports from the QuickBooks Main menu.

2. QuickBooks displays the Reports menu (see Figure 21.1). (Press F5 to access the Reports menu from the Write Checks screen, the Write Invoices screen, or any register.)

3. Press the number that corresponds to the report you want to create. When you select a report that is followed by three dots (. . .), QuickBooks displays a submenu with additional reports you can choose.

Figure 21.1 The Reports menu lists the reports you can create and print.

4. QuickBooks displays a report window. The name of the report you are creating appears in the report title. For example, if you select the Profit & Loss-report from the Reports menu, QuickBooks displays the Create Profit & Loss Statement window (Figure 21.2).

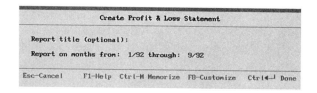

Figure 21.2 The Create Profit & Loss Statement window.

5. Type a report title (optional) and the dates the report covers. Note some reports may require additional information in the report window.

6. Press Ctrl-Enter or F10. QuickBooks searches through the transactions and displays the report.

Moving Around the Report Screen

When a report is on-screen, you may need to move around the report screen to examine the report in its entirety. Use the following keys to move around report screens:

Keys	To Move
Right arrow	One column to the right.
Left arrow	One column to the left.
Tab or Ctrl-Right arrow	One screen to the right.
Shift-Tab or Ctrl-Left arrow	One screen to the left.
Home	To the top-left corner of the report.
End	To the bottom-right corner of the report.

Printing Reports

To print reports that appear on your screen:

1. Insert blank paper in your printer. Make sure your printer is turned on and is on-line.

2. With the report displayed on your screen, press Ctrl-P.

3. QuickBooks displays the Print Report window.

4. If your printer does not appear in the Print to field, press Ctrl-L to select another printer or a disk file format (if you want to print to disk).

5. Press Enter to begin printing.

Printing a Report to a Disk File

To print a report to a disk file, follow these steps:

1. Create and display the report on-screen.

2. Press Ctrl-P to display the Print Report window.

3. At the `Print to` field, press Ctrl-L and select:

   `.TXT File`   Converts to text file for word processing.

   `.PRN File`   Creates a comma-delimited ASCII text file for database, word-processing, or spreadsheet programs.

   `.WKS File`   Creates a file that can be read by Lotus 1-2-3.

4. Press Enter.

5. QuickBooks displays the Print to Disk window. Type the DOS file name; for .TXT files, type the number of lines per page and the width.

6. Press Ctrl-Enter to begin saving the report to the file.

 **Memorized Reports**   Memorize frequently used report formats. Create the report you want to memorize and press Ctrl-M. Type a report title. Press Enter. To recall the memorized report, select the Memorized Reports option from the Reports menu, and choose it from the Memorized Reports List.

Lesson 22

Managing Your QuickBooks Files

In this lesson, you will learn how to work with more than one company file, as well as how to back up and restore company files.

Adding a Company File

QuickBooks enables you to add company files so you can maintain separate books for more than one enterprise. Each company file you add has its own Chart of Accounts, and is kept completely separate from the other company files in your system.

To add a new company file to your QuickBooks system, follow these steps:

1. Select the Set Up/Customize option from the QuickBooks Main menu.

2. From the Set Up/Customize window, choose the Select/Add a Company option.

3. QuickBooks displays the Select/Set Up Company window, shown in Figure 22.1, with a list of all company files in your QuickBooks system.

Tells you when action needs to be taken in a company file.

```
                    Select/Set Up Company

            Current Directory: C:\QBOOKS\QBDATA\
                        (77588K free)
                                                   Next Event
    Company Name              Filename   Date   Size  Scheduled

  ▶ 18Minute                  18MINUTE  9/16/92   7K  Tue   9/ 1/92
    Accounting Services       ACCOUNTI  9/ 4/92   7K  Thu   5/28/92
    CompuText                 COMPUTEX  9/ 9/92  46K  Mon   6/22/92
    Example                   EXAMPLE   6/ 2/92   3K
    Hyatt-Computers           HYATTCOM  6/15/92   3K
    LAF, Inc.                 LAF_INC   9/14/92   4K  Mon   8/18/92
    QuickPay Sample Company   QPSAMPLE  6/ 1/92  24K
    QuickWrite                QUICKWRI  6/24/92   3K
    Schmull-Rauch House       JRLEAGUE  8/14/92  87K

    Esc-Cancel      F7-Actions       F9-Set Directory        ←┘ Use
```

Indicates the date the company file was created.

Figure 22.1 The Select/Set Up Company window.

4. Press Ctrl-Ins to display the Add New Company window.

5. Complete the Add New Company window, as you learned in Lesson 2. Press Ctrl-Enter.

6. QuickBooks next displays the Creating Company File window. Make any necessary changes, and press Ctrl-Enter or F10 to add the new company file.

Selecting a Company File to Use If you have more than one company file, you need to tell QuickBooks which file you want to use when you start the program. Access the Select/Set Up Company window, as explained above, and then use the Up and Down arrow keys to move the arrow to the company file you want to use. Press Enter to access the company file.

Deleting a Company File

To delete a company file you no longer need, follow these steps:

1. Select the Set Up/Customize option from the QuickBooks Main menu.

2. Choose the Select/Add a Company option.

3. Use the arrow keys to point to the company file you want to delete.

4. Press Ctrl-Del.

5. Type Yes and press Enter to delete the company file permanently.

Deleting Company Files   When you delete a company file, QuickBooks permanently removes all the company's data from the system. Before you delete a company file, *make a backup copy.* You can restore the company file later if you need to retrieve the data.

Backing Up a Company File

A power failure or hardware malfunction can cause loss or damage to your QuickBooks company files. To protect yourself from losing data, back up your company files frequently. To back up a company file:

1. Insert a blank, formatted disk in drive A or B. (If you are backing up to your hard drive, omit this step.)

2. Select the Set Up/Customize option from the QuickBooks Main menu.

3. Press 2 to display the BackUp/Restore menu.

4. Select the Back Up Company Files option.

5. QuickBooks displays the Select Company to Back Up window. Use the Up and Down arrow keys to point to the company file you want to back up, and press Enter.

6. QuickBooks displays the Backup Directory window. Type the drive or directory to which you want to back up your company file.

7. Press Enter to begin the backup procedure.

 Backing Up from the Main Menu You can access the backup option quickly from the Main menu by pressing Ctrl-B. To back up the current company file and then exit QuickBooks, press Ctrl-E from the Main menu.

Restoring a Company File

If you lose or destroy your original company file, you can restore the file using the backup copy. To restore a company file, follow these steps:

1. Insert your backup copy in drive A or B. If your backup copy is contained on your hard disk, omit this step.

2. Select the Set Up/Customize option from the QuickBooks Main menu.

3. Press 2 to display the BackUp/Restore menu.

4. Select the Restore Company Files option.

5. QuickBooks displays the Restore Directory window. Type the drive or directory that contains your backup copy. Press Enter.

6. Use the arrow keys to point to the company file you want to restore in the Select Company File to Restore window. Press Enter to begin the restoration process.

Using Passwords

You can assign owner and bookkeeper passwords to your QuickBooks company files to prevent unauthorized access and use.

Owner and Bookkeeper Passwords   The *owner password* is the highest-security password; it enables you to access all QuickBooks activities. The *bookkeeper password* is a lower-level security password that enables access to only the activities you assign.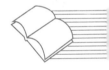

To assign passwords, follow these steps:

1. Select the Set Up/Customize option from the QuickBooks Main menu.

2. Press 4 to display the Customize Current Company menu.

3. Select the Passwords option.

4. QuickBooks displays the Set Passwords window. Type an owner password of up to 16 characters (including spaces), and press Enter.

5. If you want to assign a bookkeeper password, type a password (up to 16 characters) in the Bookkeeper password field, and press Enter.

6. To restrict access to transactions before a certain date, type that date.

7. Press Ctrl-Enter or F10.

8. To confirm the owner password, type the password and press Enter.

9. QuickBooks displays the Password Level Assignment window in which you can assign owner, bookkeeper, or no passwords to 13 different activities. (See the next section in this lesson).

Assigning Password Activities

To assign the activities you want to safeguard with a password, follow these steps:

1. At the Password Level Assignment window (shown in Figure 22.2), use the Up and Down arrow keys to point to the activity you want to protect with a password.

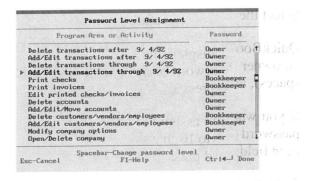

Figure 22.2 Use the Password Level Assignment window to assign passwords to QuickBooks activities.

2. Press the Spacebar to assign the owner password. Press the Spacebar again to assign the bookkeeper password. To return the setting to None Req'd (no password required), press the Spacebar a third time.

3. Continue assigning passwords to activities; once finished, press Ctrl-Enter or F10 to save the password settings.

Forgotten Passwords Don't forget your password. If you don't enter the correct password, you may not be able to access your company file or perform activities. Call an Intuit Technical Support specialist for help if you lose your password.

Lesson 23

Customizing QuickBooks

In this lesson, you will learn how to customize your company file and the QuickBooks program.

Setting Company Options

When you install QuickBooks, the program sets company and program options that control how you enter transactions, and how the program works for you. You can change any company or program option so QuickBooks meets your needs. *Company options* control the way QuickBooks works in the current company file. To set company options, follow these steps:

1. Select Set Up/Customize from the Main menu.

2. Press 4 to display the Customize Current Company menu.

3. Select Options to display the Customize Options window shown in Figure 23.1.

4. Press Ctrl-L at the Invoice type field, and select the type of invoice you use.

Press Tab to move from option to option.

```
          Customize Options for 10MINUTE

1. ◆Invoice type   (Service/Professional/Product): Service
2. Receive payments from customers on Open
     item or Balance forward basis        (O/B): B
3. Require item codes on invoice line items (Y/N): Y
4. Default number of days between DATE and
     PAY DATE in Accounts Payable        (0-99): 10
5. Sales tax collected is payable Monthly,
     Quarterly, or Annually             (M/Q/A): M
6. Require account on all transactions      (Y/N): Y
7. Project tracking on                      (Y/N): N
8. Extra message line on checks             (Y/N): N
9. Change check dates to the date printed   (Y/N): N
10. Print full detail on voucher checks     (Y/N): N
11. Show Memo/Account/Both in registers    (M/A/B): B
12. Show lowest subaccounts/subprojects only (Y/N): N
13. Show account Name/Desc/Both in reports (N/D/B): B
14. Warn if a check number is reused        (Y/N): Y
15. Warn if an invoice number is reused     (Y/N): Y

Esc-Cancel          F1-Help           Ctrl◄─┘ Done
```

Figure 23.1   Use the Customize Options window to set company options for the current company file.

5. Press Tab to move the cursor from option to option. Set the company options to your personal preference.

6. Press Ctrl-Enter or F10 to save the settings.

Setting Program Options

Program options control the way several QuickBooks features work. To set program options, follow these steps:

1. Select Set Up/Customize from the Main menu.

2. Press 5 to choose Customize QuickBooks, and then select Options.

3. QuickBooks displays the Program Options window (see Figure 23.2).

4. Press Tab to move the cursor from option to option. Set the program options to your personal preference.

159

```
                    Program Options

  1. QuickTrainer lag: Short/Long/Off (S/L/O): S
  2. Beep when recording and memorizing (Y/N): N
  3. Request confirmation (for example,
        when changing the Register)    (Y/N): Y
  4. MM/DD/YY or DD/MM/YY date format    (M/D): M
  5. Days in advance to remind of scheduled
        bills, invoices, and groups  (0-30): 3
  6. Bizminder active                    (Y/N): N
  7. 43 line register/reports (EGA,VGA) (Y/N): N
  8. On new checks/invoices, start with the
        Payee/customer or Date field  (P/D): P
  9. Double-click speed for mouse (0 turns
        mouse off)                     (0-9): 4
 10. Warn to deposit payments received  (Y/N): N

 Esc-Cancel          F1-Help          Ctrl◄─┘ Done
```

Figure 23.2 The Program Options window.

5. Press Ctrl-Enter or F10 to save the settings.

Using Bizminder

Bizminder is QuickBooks' reminder system that checks your company files and displays messages each time you start your computer. Bizminder reminds you about actions you need to take (such as printing checks, paying bills, or executing transaction groups), and also alerts you to over-due customer invoices.

When you install QuickBooks, the program asks if you want to install Bizminder. If you answer Yes, Bizminder executes each time you turn on your computer, and displays a message. Press Enter to remove the Bizminder message and return to DOS.

This lesson concludes your course through the *10 Minute Guide to QuickBooks.*

Index

161

balance forward method (payment
application method), 116
balance sheet accounts, 28,
140-146
balances
checking account, 16
Credit Card register,
adjusting, 139
opening, 92, 143
bank statement, 90-92
bills, 127-130
Bizminder, 160
bookkeeper password, 155

C

calculated pay date (bills), 128
calculating transactions (split), 73
calculator, 24-26
Calculator option, 24
chain calculations, 26
Chart of Accounts, 10, 28-36
Chart of Accounts Help
window, 20
Chart of Accounts option, 15, 29
Chart Of Accounts window, 12,
15, 29
Check register, 61-63
checks, 50-51, 69-70
printing, 70
scrolling, 68
transactions, 63-68, 78-79
see also checking account
Check Register option, 62
Checkbook option, 45
checking account, 140
balance, 16, 143
creating, 14-16
deposits, 119
reconciling, 89-95
checks, 46-48
deleting, 50-51
editing, 48-50
finding, 50

memorized, 79-80
numbering, 58
postdated, 57
printing, 53-60
reviewing, 48-50
voiding, 51, 69-70
Choose Bills to Pay window, 133
Clear option, 26
Combine option, 36
combining accounts, 35-36
commands, selecting, 5
company files, 10-14, 151-156
company lists, 10, 37-43
Company Lists option, 39
company options, 158-159
converting Quicken data to
QuickBooks, 13-18
copying
calculations, 27
transactions, split, 73
Create Opening Balance
Adjustment window, 95
creating
checking account, 14-16
reports, 147-148
subaccounts, 32
credit card account, 134-139
Credit Card register, 137-139
Credit Card Statement Information
window, 138
credit memos, 117
Current Asset account
register, 145
Customer Aging Status
Schedule, 112
customer list, 37-38
customization, 158-160
Customize Options window, 158

D

dates
bills, calculated pay date, 128
changing, check writing, 46

M

Main menu, 2
Make Credit Card Payment
    window, 139
Make Deposits option, 119
marking cleared transactions, 93
Memorize Transaction option, 78
memorized checks, recalling, 80
Memorized Reports option, 150
memorizing
    bills, 129
    checks, 79
    credit card transactions, 137
    invoices, 104
    transactions, 77-82
menus, 3-5
messages, QuickTrainer, 1
mouse, 3, 6-7
moving
    accounts, 34-35
    in report screen, 149
    subaccounts to higher-level
        account, 35

N–O

numbering
    checks, 58
    invoices, 111

open item method (payment
    application method), 116
opening balances, 16, 92, 143
options, selecting, 3-7
ordering supplies, 52-53, 106
overpayments, 117
overwriting transactions, 79
owner's equity, 29
owner's equity account, 141, 143

P

Password Level Assignment
    window, 156
passwords, 155-156
Passwords option, 156
Pay Bills option, 130
Pay Vendors window, 130
payee list, 38
payment application methods, 116
payment terms list, 38
payments, 114-118, 132-133
payments methods list, 39
percentages, 26
postdated checks, printing, 57
Preparing to Record Checks
    window, 132
preprinted checks, ordering, 52-53
Print Checks option, 53
Print Checks window, 54
Print Invoices option, 107
Print Invoices window, 107
Print List window, 43
Print option, 43
Print Reconciliation Report
    window, 94
Print Report window, 150
Print Statements option, 113
Print Statements window, 113
Print Supplies Order Form
    option, 52
Print to Disk window, 150
printers, 17-18
    checks, 52
    invoices, aligning, 108-111
    laser, printing checks, 55-56
    not listed, 18
    positioning checks, 53-56
    selecting, 17
printing, 17-18
    Chart of Accounts, 36
    Check Register, 70
    checks, 56-60

company lists, 42-43
deposit summary, 120
invoices, 107-112
order form (checks), 52
reconciliation report, 94
reports, 149-150
statements, 112-113
Printing view, 99
.PRN file format, 150
program options, 159-160
Program Options window, 160
projects, 38
  bills, 129
  check transactions, 47
  invoice transactions, 101
pull-down menus, 3-5

Q

Quick keys, 3, 5
QuickBooks
  exiting, 8-9
  starting, 1-2
Quicken, converting data to
    QuickBooks, 13-18
QuickTrainer, 1-2, 21

R

Recall Transaction option, 79
recalling memorized items, 79-80
Receive Payments option, 114
Receive Payments screen, 114-115
Reconcile option, 90
Reconcile Register with Bank
    Statement window, 90
Reconcile/Pay option, 137
reconciliation report, 94
RECONCILIATION
    SUMMARY, 94
Reconciliation Summary, credit
    card account, 139

reconciling
  checking account, 89-95
  credit card account, 137-139
recording
  invoices, 103-104
  payments, 118
  transactions, selecting account,
    144-145
registers
  Accounts Payable, *see*
    Accounts Payable register
  Accounts Receivable, *see*
    Accounts Receivable register
  Credit Card, *see* Credit Card
    register
reports, 94, 112, 147-150
Restore Company Files
    option, 155
Restore Directory window, 155

S

screens
  Help, 19
  Receive Payments, 114-115
  report, 149
  Write Checks, *see* Write
    Checks screen
scrolling, 7
  Check Register, 68
  Write Checks screen, 48-50
Select Company to Back Up
    window, 154
Select List window, 39
Select/Add a Company option,
    11, 151
selecting
  accounts, recording
    transactions, 144-145
  checks, printing, 59, 60
  commands, keyboards, 5
  company files, 152
  invoices, printing, 112